Places of interest around our coast

see Information pages
for further details

1 Westray, Orkneys
2 North Hoy, Orkneys
3 Dunnet Head, Scottish Highlands
4 Dornoch Firth, Scottish Highlands
5 Cromarty Firth, Scottish Highlands
6 Culbin Sands, Grampian
7 Sands of Forvie, Grampian
8 Tentsmuir Point, Fife
9 Bass Rock, Lothian
10 St Abbs Head, Borders
11 Lindisfarne, Northumberland
12 Farne Islands, Northumberland
13 Teeside, Cleveland
14 Flamborough Head and Bempton Cliffs, Humberside
15 Spurn Point, Humberside
16 Gibraltar Point, Lincolnshire
17 Wash, Lincolnshire/Norfolk
18 Hunstanton, Norfolk
19 Scolt Head, Norfolk
20 Blakeney Point, Norfolk
21 Orfordness, Suffolk
22 Walton-on-the-Naze, Essex
23 North Kent Marshes, Kent
24 Sandwich Bay, Kent

25 Dungeness, Kent
26 Beachy Head, Sussex
27 Seven Sisters, Sussex
28 Portsmouth, Langstone, Chichester Harbours,
   Hampshire/Sussex
29 Hurst Point, Hampshire
30 The Needles, Isle of Wight
31 Purbeck Cliffs, Dorset
32 Lulworth Cove, Dorset
33 Chesil Beach, Dorset
34 Exe Estuary, Devon
35 Dawlish Warren, Devon
36 Slapton Sands, Devon
37 Start Point, Devon
38 Fal Estuary, Cornwall
39 Lizard, Cornwall
40 Cornwall Coast Path, Cornwall
41 Bude, Cornwall
42 Welcombe and Marshland Reserve, Devon
43 Braunton Burrows, Devon
44 Bridgwater Bay, Somerset
45 Slimbridge, Gloucester
46 Dunraven, Glamorgan
47 Gower Peninsula, Glamorgan
48 Whiteford Burrows, Glamorgan
49 Pembroke Coast Path, Dyfed

50 Skomer Island, Dyfed
51 St Davids Head, Dyfed
52 Cors Fochno, Dyfed
53 Newborough Warren, Gwynedd
54 Menai Straits, Gwynedd
55 South Stack, Gwynedd
56 Dee Estuary, Clwyd/Merseyside
57 Ainsdale, Merseyside
58 Morecambe Bay, Lancashire/Cumbria
59 St Bees Head, Cumbria
60 Caerlaverock, Dumfries
61 Mull of Galloway, Galloway
62 South Ardnamurchan Coast, Argyll
63 Loch Scavaig, Skye
64 Giant's Causeway, Antrim
65 Dingle Bay, Kerry

Discovering
the
Countryside
with
David
Bellamy

Hamlyn
London · New York · Sydney · Toronto

Coastal Walks

Acknowledgements

Artwork
Norman Arlott, 45 (from *RSPB Guide to Birdwatching*); John Busby (from
Seabirds : their biology and ecology); Peter Crump 14–15; Kim Ludlow 30, 49, 88,
102; James Nicholls (from *The Hamlyn Guide to the Seashore and Shallow Seas of
Britain and Europe*).

Photographs
NHPA – R. W. S. Knightbridge 43. All other photographs by Peter Loughran.

Published by
The Hamlyn Publishing Group Limited
London · New York · Sydney · Toronto
Astronaut House, Feltham, Middlesex, England

© The Hamlyn Publishing Group Limited 1982
ISBN 0 600 35588 8

Printed in Great Britain

The Publishers and David Bellamy would like to thank the following organisations for their help in preparing this book.

Royal Society for Nature Conservation
Hampshire and Isle of Wight Naturalists' Trust
Dunraven Heritage Coastal Park
Lincolnshire and South Humberside Trust for Nature Conservation

In particular we would like to express our gratitude to the gallant team of experts: David Billett, Mary Gillham, John Barrett, Ian Mercer and Ted Smith, whose hospitality, enthusiasm and vast knowledge of our countryside is only hinted at in these pages.

Country Code
Whenever and wherever you are out walking, please follow these simple rules:
- Guard against risk of fire
- Close all gates behind you, especially those at cattle grids, etc.
- Keep dogs under control
- Keep to paths across farmland – you have no right of way over surrounding land
- Avoid damaging fences, hedges and walls
- Leave no litter   take it away with you
- Safeguard water supplies
- Protect wildlife, plants and trees – do not pick flowers, leave them for others to enjoy
- Drive carefully on country roads
- Respect the life of the countryside – and you will be welcomed.

The seashore can be a dangerous place so if you are planning to make a trip, remember:
- Always check the tide tables and the weather reports
- Always tell other people where you are going, and don't go on your own unless it is unavoidable
- Dress properly; it can get mighty cold and the rocks are very slippery. I find a pair of training shoes with good soles ideal for scrambling about
- A trip to the local museum is always a good idea when planning your trip and it can save an awful lot of your precious holiday time
- Never, repeat never, collect a live animal or plant. When it comes to shells and other flotsam, only collect what you need. There are others following in your footsteps.

Foreword

'Oh, I do like to be beside the seaside!' I have said it, shouted and even sung it, and what is more I really do mean it. There is no better place for a budding naturalist to get his or her feet wet than the seashores of Britain. Just look at a map of the British Isles – there's lots of coastline in relation to land area. That is one of the advantages of living on an island, but even better, just look at all the indentations; there are miles and miles of excitement and always something more to look at just around the corner. Add to this the varied geology of Britain ranging from the hard, acidic granites to the soft, erodable limestones and all the rock types in-between, all exposed to the force of the waves; the large rivers depositing their products of erosion; onshore currents washing material from one area to another; the fact that the west coast is bathed by the warm balmy waters of the North Atlantic Drift and the east faces the chilling winds coming down clear across from the Arctic and the Urals; and what have you got: diversity and that is the spice of life.

If any of you are now saying, 'Oh dear, diversity – that means there is going to be lots of different things to sort out, lots of names to learn.' Please hold on, for despite this diversity all our coasts have one thing in common: tides; and it is the tidal cycle that adds order to what would otherwise be a very confusing world. Every day, twice a day, the tide comes in and goes back out again and as it does this it exposes and resubmerges an area which is called the littoral zone. Any plant or animal living between the tides has got to put up with these drastic changes in its home environment. Add to this constant cycle the effect of crashing waves, torrential rain, biting winds, hot summer sun and cold winter frosts and you have a very harsh habitat. The end result is that very few plants and animals, albeit from a wide range of groups, have evolved to be successful denizens of the littoral zone.

I reckon if you learn to identify forty or so different plants and animals that wherever you might be on the British coast you should be able to feel at home. You then will not only be meeting with 'old friends' but will immediately notice what is new and exciting. In other words, a little knowledge of the most common and abundant members of our seashore life will open the doors to the diversity of life hiding in the rock pools and along the beach. But don't forget to look out for all the marvellous birds that take advantage of all these sources of food, especially along our lovely muddy estuaries. Many of them have travelled thousands of miles to enjoy the wealth of plant and animal life around our shores.

The coastline also has a tremendously interesting group of land plants growing along its higher reaches and one of the most exciting things a natural historian can do, after he has had a good splash around down in the littoral zone, is to discover how these plants have colonised the shore. To see how this actually happens we went on a walk along a shingle beach and across a sand dune system where the grasses have actually helped to mould their own environment.

The way that I made my first steps towards understanding the natural history of the British countryside was to go out into the field with a local expert and soak up some of his or her enthusiasm and local knowledge. This is exactly what we have tried to do in this book and all the others in the series. We have gone out with local experts and let them introduce us to their 'home patch' and show us some of the things that make the study of their particular area so absorbing. It was very exciting and I learnt a tremendous amount. Some of the walks have taken place on reserves managed by conservation trusts and all our guides are active members of these trusts. So if you want to learn more about your own local scene why don't you join your county or regional conservation trust. They do a tremendous amount of valuable work and you will be surprised how, after going along to some of their field meetings and rubbing shoulders with them, you too will soon become an expert yourself.

Good beachcombing

Discovering the Countryside with David Bellamy Coastal Walks

Contents

Bellamy's Seaside

Coastal Marshes and Estuaries

Photography by Peter Loughran

Sea Cliffs

Shingle Beaches

Rocky Shorelines

Sand Dunes

Bellamy's Seaside

On a day trip to the sea? Fed up with building sand castles? Well, take a look along the beach and you will be surprised what you will find in the way of marine life. I can hear you saying, 'What, any old beach?'. To answer that question I went to one of the nearest stretches of shoreline from my home in County Durham. It is nothing at all special – I would even say that it is rather ugly and yet I spent a whole day happily dabbling around and I will go back again and again.

Here I am just about to get my feet wet beside a rock pool at the seaside.

The tides

Probably the most conspicuous feature of any seashore around our coasts is the daily rise and fall of the tides. These are caused by the gravitational pull of the moon and the sun. A high or low tide occurs approximately every twelve hours and at least one period in every month the tide reaches its maximum flow and ebb. This happens about two days after a full moon and a new moon and is called a *spring tide*, although it bears no relationship to that particular season of the year. Between the periods of the spring tides there is a time when the ebb and flow of the water is at a minimum; this is the time of *neap tides*. This variation in the tidal range is a result of differences in the alignment of the moon and the sun in relation to the earth. At a new moon and a full moon, the sun and the moon are pulling together almost in a straight line so that the tidal ranges are greater. During neap tides the sun and the moon are less aligned and may be at right angles, therefore reducing their combined effects. In addition there is also an annual rhythm to this, since at the equinoxes in September and March the sun and the moon pull exactly in a straight line, giving exceptionally large spring tides.

The effect of these tides on the shore life is considerable as some areas are obviously covered and uncovered by the sea every 12 hours, whilst higher points on the shore may be only covered for a few days each month, during spring tides. Those animals which can withstand exposure to the air with all its attendant variables are to be found at the top of the shore, and those that can only tolerate a small amount of exposure are found lower down. This basic effect produces a zoning of the plants and animals which can clearly be seen on many shorelines. This *zonation* is at its most obvious on rocky shores but is also present on muddy and sandy shores. On an exposed shore the various zones are broader than on a sheltered shore. This is because of the way in which wave and wind action serves to extend the influence of sea water up the shore beyond the point that it would have reached if the water was still.

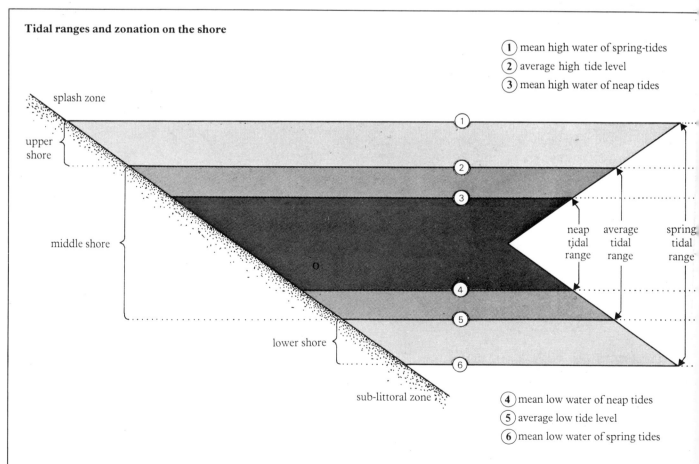

Tidal ranges and zonation on the shore

1. mean high water of spring-tides
2. average high tide level
3. mean high water of neap tides

splash zone

upper shore

middle shore

lower shore

sub-littoral zone

neap tidal range   average tidal range   spring tidal range

4. mean low water of neap tides
5. average low tide level
6. mean low water of spring tides

Bellamy's forty seaside animals and plants :

Plants

ALGAE

Green Seaweeds
  Sea Lettuce *Ulva lactuca*
  Intestine Weed *Enteromorpha intestinalis*

Brown Seaweeds
  Channelled Wrack *Pelvetia canaliculata*
  Spiral Wrack *Fucus spiralis*
  Bladder Wrack *Fucus vesiculosus*
  Serrated Wrack *Fucus serratus*
  Smoothed-stalked Kelp *Laminaria digitata*
  Rough-stalked Kelp *Laminaria hyperborea*
  Crinkled Kelp *Laminaria saccharina*

Red Seaweeds
  Dulse *Rhodymenia palmata*
  Purple Laver *Porphyra umbilicalis*

Animals

PORIFERA — SPONGES
Demospongiae
  Breadcrumb Sponge *Halichondria panicea*

CNIDARIA
Hydrozoa
  Sea Fir *Gonothyraea loveni*

Scyphozoa – Jellyfish
  Common Jellyfish *Aurelia aurita*

Anthozoa – Sea Anemones
  Beadlet *Actinia equina*
  Snakelocks *Anemonia sulcata*

ANNELIDA — SEGMENTED WORMS
Polychaeta – Bristle worms
  Ragworm *Nereis virens*
  Green Paddleworm *Eulalia viridis*
  Spirorbis borealis

MOLLUSCA
Gastropoda – Snails and Slugs
  Limpet *Patella vulgata*
  topshells *Gibbula, Monodonta*
  winkles *Littorina*
  Dogwelk *Nucella lapillus*
Bivalvia
  Mussel *Mytilus edulis*
  Common Cockle *Cerastoderma edule*
  Razor shell *Ensis siliqua*

ARTHROPODA
Crustacea
  Acorn Barnacle *Balanus balanoides*
  Sand-hopper *Orchestia gammarella*
  Common Shrimp *Crangon vulgaris*
  Broad-clawed Porcelain Crab *Porcellana platycheles*
  Hermit Crab *Eupagurus bernhardus*
  Shore Crab *Carcinus maenas*

ECTOPROCTA
Gymnolaemata
  Sea mat *Membranipora membranacea*

ECHINODERMATA
Asteroidea – Starfishes
  Common Starfish *Asterias rubens*
Ophiuroidea – Brittle Stars
  Common Brittle-Star *Ophiothrix fragilis*
Echinoidea – Sea Urchins
  Edible Sea Urchin *Echinus esculentus*
  Sea-potato *Echinocardium cordatum*

CHORDATA
Ascidiacea
  Star Ascidian *Botryllus schlosseri*
VERTEBRATA
Osteichthyes – Bony fishes
blennies *Blennius*
gobies *Gobius*

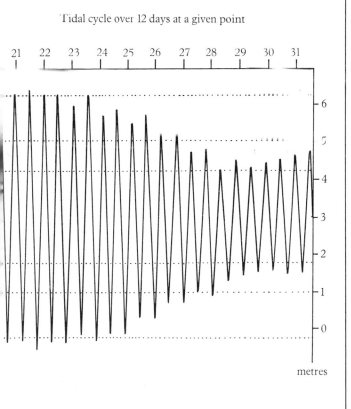

Tidal cycle over 12 days at a given point

21 22 23 24 25 26 27 28 29 30 31

metres

Bellamy's Seaside

I have often said that given any piece of our seashore, a naturalist should be able to find enough to keep him or herself busy for hours without moving more than one hundred metres. So, today, I have come to prove it, and the area I have chosen is one of the less salubrious stretches of the coastline of the North East of England. If the Industrial Revolution didn't actually start here, most of its developments happened hereabouts. Ever since industrial pollution was invented this stretch of beach has had more than its fair share and today it lies close to the mouth of one of the world's busiest industrial rivers.

The shoreline is not a pretty site. The beach, which was originally formed of magnesium limestone, is now covered with debris of varying sorts: concrete, house bricks, pieces of glass, wood and the inevitable plastic, you name it and it's here. All this is backed by a gaunt Victorian seawall. Yet in amongst all the human bric-a-brac, I guarantee that there will be many living things of great interest.

I always start at the strand line, for there, in amongst all the jetsam that has been washed up, I can usually find specimens of everything I will see lower down the beach. What is more, this is the one place in which collecting the odd specimen to take home will do no harm because all the things here have come to the end of their natural life span. They have all died and have been dumped high and dry by the tide. So you can have enormous fun here, searching for the best piece of seaweed or the best shell for your collection. But please, only take what you want because you must remember that you are not the only pebble on the beach, there will be plenty of other beach-combers coming along and they do not want to be disappointed.

Here is a great mass of seaweed all tangled up together. There are nine different sorts in all, the most abundant being a dull brown colour. Seaweeds are the common term for the marine algae, and the 'browns' are by far the largest and most common on our cool temperate shores.

These must be the commonest of them all: the wracks; everyone knows these. They are the seaweeds that aunty always brings back from her day at the sea to act as a barometer: wet and slippery when wet; dry and brittle to the touch when dry.

Whether or not you believe in their wea-ther forecasting properties, a close look at a brown seaweed will reveal that it is quite unlike your average garden plant in that it is not divided into root, stem and leaf. Each consists of a single plant body – a thallus. They are fixed to rocks or, in some cases, pebbles, by a holdfast which may be disc shaped, like a sucker, or branch-like, as in the root of a land plant. One major difference is that true roots penetrate down into the substrata whereas the branches of the hold-

fast can only stick on to the surface. Another difference is that the holdfast branches dichotomously, which means that at each branch point it divides into two equal halves. Compare the branching of a holdfast with that of the root or come to that, the shoots of a garden plant and you will find that the branching in the latter is much more complex and, in biological terms, much more advanced. The seaweeds were doing their thing in the seas of the world millions of years before there were any land plants. I defy you to find a dichotomously branched plant growing in your garden. I also defy you to find seaweeds uninteresting once you have taken a close look and learnt about their weird ways of life.

Here is a piece of Spiral Wrack, *Fucus spiralis*, and, yes, it is in fruit, there on the end of each branch is a swollen portion. If I hold it up to the light each swelling looks as if it has got a bad dose of measles. Each of these is a fertile conceptacle and the spots are the reproductive organs which either contain sperm or eggs. In this case they have already been released into the sea and some of the eggs will have been fertilised and some of them will have been carried out to sea. If they are lucky, they will end up on a bare piece of rock where they can develop into a new wrack plant. If you want to find out all about their reproduction you will need a microscope and a lot of patience. However, even with them high and dry on the strand line it is easy to see the differences between the three main species: Spiral Wrack is a small brown seaweed with a spiral twist to it. Bladder Wrack is the one with double 'poppers', one on each side of the thick mid rib. But don't muddle the 'popper floats' up with the fertile conceptacles. Serrated Wrack is the largest of the three which, as its name suggests, has a serrated edge to the blade, rather like a saw. Now we have got these basic differences plugged into our minds, a trip down the beach should let us into the secrets of their ecology, the way they live.

However, here there is no need to move all that far because flanking the beach at this point is a magnificent seawall, as Victorian as its makers, a masterpiece of the mason's art, fashioned from beautifully shaped blocks of stone. This wall will weather anything that the North Sea can throw at it for many centuries to come and the local marine life has cashed in on this fact and made it their home. From a distance it looks as if someone has been along with a gigantic brush painting broad horizontal stripes, with lurid green at the very top then four shades of brown and finally at the bottom a lovely mixture of deep reds and purples. This is the classic zonation of the normally gently sloping seashore truncated into some 2·6 metres of vertical seawall. Why, I could give a whole term's degree course in marine biology without moving away from this wall. Even though it is entirely man made, highly polluted and on the east coast of England which is not famed for its marine biological interest. A closer look at the wall shows that the zonation is much more complex than it appears at first. At the top there is a mixture of green seaweeds, which includes one which can only be described as 'dirty green'. Close up it looks like a series of little bladders which may have a silvery appearance due to trapped air. This is *Prasiola stipitata* (sorry about the name it doesn't have an English one!). It is a plant which appears to thrive on organic pollution for its natural habitat is the splash zone of rocks in seabird colonies. Apparently human sewage is as rich in phosphates and nitrates as are seabird droppings, for the *Prasiola* is certainly doing well here.

Mixed in with this are masses of a red seaweed called *Porphyra umbilicalis*. This is the famous Laver Bread which makes the traditional Welsh breakfast so tasty; not that I would collect it for eating along this shoreline.

In amongst this upper zone is the first of the wracks, the small but very tough Channelled Wrack. This is easily identified by the fact that the blades are channelled rather like a rolled human tongue. If you are unable to roll your tongue, then find someone who can and check out the features of *Pelvetia canaliculata*.

Below this rather mixed zone the three larger wracks have established themselves into clear bands. Firstly, there is Spiral Wrack, *Fucus spiralis*, then below that is the Bladder Wrack, *Fucus vesiculosus* and then at the bottom is the Serrated Wrack, *Fucus serratus*. A close look will show you that in the centre of each zone, each species of seaweed forms a monoculture in which no other seaweed can grow. In such a crowded place the competition is going to be very fierce and only the fittest will survive. It would appear that evolution has fitted each sort of wrack to thrive best in one particular tidal range. Within that range, however broad or narrow, that particular species will be able to reign supreme, filling all the available habitat space. Only at the margins of each zone is there enough room for other species to find space for their holdfasts.

When you are next down at the seaside take a close look at these seaweeds, poke about in amongst the wracks and try to prove me right or wrong. As you do this you will learn a lot about the plants themselves. For a start, they will all feel very slippery and are certainly not very nice to walk about on, but without that slippum the plants would be scraped to bits by the waves which wash them back and forth over the rocks. This slippum is produced by the plant and that takes energy and no plant is going to waste energy just to make the occasional budding algologist fall flat on his face. One second fact that becomes very obvious is that in the crowded world of the seaweed zones there is little or no room for a new plant, even of the same species, to get a foothold. One important thing for all organisms that live fixed to one spot in a crowded world is the need for an efficient method of dispersal of their young. Each year countless billions of fertilised seaweed eggs go to waste carried to the wrong place by the vagaries of wind and tide. They are either eaten or fall onto stony ground in the sense of the biblical parable. However, the few that survive are sufficient to fill the spaces on the shore vacated by the death of other plants.

The last zone at the foot of the seawall is a livid red-purple colour, covered with a mixture of several different types of red seaweed. Of all the types of seaweed, the 'reds' are amongst the most difficult to identify so at this juncture I think we will just say that they are a lovely colour and pass on down the shore.

The seaweed zonation we have seen on the wall is also present on the shore itself but in a much more extended form as the width of each zone is dependent on the angle of the slope. So in order to see the 'red' zone I will have to do a lot of walking . . . oops! I have slipped into a rock pool. The zonation on the beach is also a much less regular business! The seawall had a relatively even surface whereas here, the slope is very uneven with deep pools and rocks sticking up in-between. The main factor determining the zonation is the fluctuation of the tide in relation to the point on which seaweed is trying to grow. . . . there I go slipping into another pool. Despite these irregularities the zonation is there and each of the main types of wrack faithfully adheres to its own special environment.

The seashore is a very special place and should be treated with the utmost respect: slippery rocks and a turning tide can land the unwary in all sorts of trouble. You should always check the state of the tide before you venture on to the beach and, however interesting you find the terrain and its inhabitants, always remember that tides have no respect for scholarship. I always like to follow the tide down and finish my study just after low water. It is all too easy on a rising tide to linger at a particular spot for just too long and find yourself cut off with, at the very least, a wet route to safety above the high tide mark.

Today, I have not followed my golden rule and the tide is already on the turn and I am going to have to be careful. Here I am close to the low tide mark and it must be a neap tide because the water is still lapping around the lower zones of the Serrated Wrack and the large plants of the next zone are only just protruding above the water. However, here in a large rock pool, which is in places almost a metre deep, all is revealed. The pool is almost filled with a tangle of kelp and I can see three different species from the edge here. A tangle of kelp! Please excuse a rather in-joke, you see the other common name for the kelps is 'tangles'. If you have never smelt the tangle of the isles then take it from me that it is the aroma of seaweed. The kelps boast among their numbers not only the largest seaweed around the coast of Britain but also the largest seaweed in the world.

The two which are most abundant in my pool are the Smooth-stalked Kelp, *Laminaria digitata*, and the Rough-stalked Kelp, *Laminaria hyperborea*. Both consist of a large well-branched (always dichotomously) holdfast, a long flexible stalk or stipe and a rather hand-like blade. There is one with last year's blade, all tattered and torn, still attached to the new one that has developed this season. The kelps are perennial plants and the holdfast and stipe increase in size throughout their life while a brand new blade is produced each year. Around our coasts, the Rough-stalked Kelp lives the longest and can become a very large plant. What is more, it is possible to tell how old they are. Take a holdfast, remembering that there are plenty washed up on the strand line so there is no need to damage a living plant, and cut it in half length ways. You will probably need a strong penknife to do this. It will now be easy to see that the branches of the hold-fast come off from the stipe in a series of levels or whorls. Very roughly the number of branch levels gives you the age of the plant in years. If you inspect the cut surface you have made you should find that each branch level is marked out within the stipe tissue by a dark line. These are like annual rings in a tree trunk and counting them will give you a more accurate measure of the age of the plant. But please be careful because false lines not connected with a branch level can lead you astray. It is the number of branch levels that counts and not the number of branches, so be careful and if you find one which is more than 15 years of age, then you are either very lucky or you have made a mistake.

The Rough-stalked Kelp always stands out from the others by the fact that its stipe is covered with a sock of red seaweeds. The knobbly surface of the stalk of this kelp provides a safe anchorage for epiphytes and the fascinating thing is that these grow in distinct zones along the stipe.

The commonest epiphyte hereabouts on the kelp's stipe is *Rhodymenia palmata*, the Edible Dulse, a lovely chewy seaweed (but please do not try and eat it along these polluted waters). Although it comes in a variety of shapes and sizes it can often be picked out by its dark red colour, producing deep purple reflections. Another epiphyte is *Ptilota plumosa*, this seaweed has repeatedly branched

Rocky shoreline exposed at low tide. The rocks in the foreground are covered with the glistening bodies of many anemones, their tentacles retracted, waiting for the tide to return.

A rock pool full of a tangle of kelp. The crinkled fronds of *Laminaria saccharina* are floating about here, with the great sprawling hand-like fronds of *Laminaria digitata*.

A whole degree course in marine biology on one exposed, rather polluted section of seawall. The broad brush strokes of algae clearly show the shore zonation: green seaweeds at the top followed by *Pelvetia canaliculata*, *Fucus spiralis*, *Fucus vesiculosus*, **and** *Fucus serratus*, with the red seaweeds becoming increasingly prominent towards the base. See the opposite page for a closer look at some better specimens of the important brown seaweeds.

Channelled Wrack, *Pelvetia canaliculata.* The tips of the frond in the centre are swollen to form reproductive bodies. This seaweed is found on the upper shore.

Spiral Wrack, *Fucus spiralis.* The tips are swollen conceptacles and the bad dose of 'measles' are the reproductive organs, which either contain sperm or eggs.

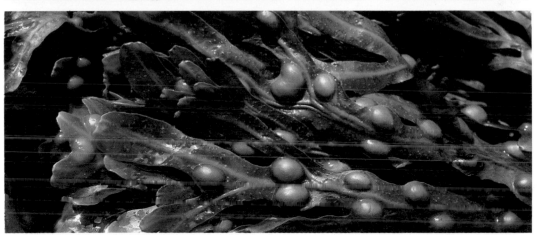

Bladder Wrack, *Fucus vesiculosus.* The 'poppers' on either side of the mid-rib are air-bladders which add buoyancy to the seaweed. This is a typical plant of the middle shore.

Serrated Wrack, *Fucus serratus.* The toothed edge of this seaweed of the lower middle shore makes it easy to identify.

fronds which give it the appearance of a bird's feather. Then there is *Membranoptera alata*, a very descriptive name for a beautiful plant, each one of which consists of a dark red midrib fringed with a transparent membrane-like blade. Often growing close to the holdfast are the exquisite fronds of *Phycodrys rubens*, this plant looks like almost transparent oak leaves, or in some forms they are lobed so as to resemble the leaves of holly. Please don't get this one muddled up with *Delesseria sanguinea*, which produces much larger transparent leaf-like fronds, which resemble neither the leaves of oak or holly.

But now I have got my feet wet I am going to explore the pool in a bit more depth. . . . Ooh, it's cold, but that's what the large seaweeds really like. The warm balmy waters of the tropics may be okay for coral reefs but they are death to the large seaweeds, which only thrive in the cool temperate waters. So much so that many of our seaweeds put on much of their growth and complete their reproduction in the cooler waters of spring. One reason why a seaweed hunt is always best at Easter.

It is lovely and slippery, sloshing about in amongst all the kelps and yes, I have found

The red seaweeds are certainly not the easiest of plants when it comes to correct identification. You will need a good guide, a lens or microscope and a lot of patience, but believe you me it is well worth while. I got hooked on the seaweed bug whilst on a course at the Dale Fort Field Centre in Pembrokeshire run by John Barrett, who will be looking at some of our more common marine animals on another walk.

Even without names, the red seaweeds that you can collect from the strand line provide hours of interest and before we leave the beach I will show you what to do with them.

A living-graph. This collection of Rough-Stalked Kelps (*Laminaria hyperborea*) shows the typical growth pattern of the kelps. The older ones on the right-hand side of the 'graph' have still got their collection of epiphytic red seaweeds attached to the stalk. The holdfasts also will have an exciting array of plants and animals living in them. This collection of kelps for our growth curve were all washed up, so don't go out and pull up any of these super seaweeds.

the third of the common kelps: *Laminaria saccharina*. This one, like the others, has a branched holdfast and then a thin short stipe leading to a great flamboyant undivided blade which is crinkled down the middle, rather like a modern with-it dress shirt. These can grow up to 2·4 metres in length but, of course, here in a rock pool, growth will be more difficult due to all the bashing about by the waves.

You know we humans are very lucky. We visit the seashore when we want to and when the weather cuts up rough or it gets too cold we can nip off home. Not so for the creatures of the sea, they have to stay put and the ones that live on the shore have to put up with the roughest, toughest environment on earth. Think about it. When the tide is out in the summer up goes the temperature, the water evaporates and you are covered in a crust of salt. There is some around the edge of our rock pool. No wonder the green seaweed looks so anaemic. Next moment it is pouring with rain and you are washed clean with almost pure distilled water. In winter exactly the opposite happens: down comes the rain and a quick snap of frost freezes you solid, then back comes the tide and you are thawed out in salty water. What a way of life, no wonder the greatest diversity of the shoreline is found in the deeper rock pools, where at least some of these fluctuations are smoothed out.

What else can I find. Well, at the moment all the fronds of these common kelps are lying as it were, flat on their faces, all mixed up. When the tide comes in the buoyant salt water will bring them all to attention and they will float upright in the swell. The best way to see this is to join the British or Scottish Sub Aqua Club and learn to dive and look to the waters. I well remember my amazement at swimming through the kelp 'forest' with all the stipes erect and the fronds displayed to advantage intercepting the dappled rays of the sun. I also remember how amazed I was when one of the kelps, which I had grabbed to steady myself in the swell, came off in my hand. Well, it didn't come off, it came up, holdfast, substrate and all. It was attached, not to solid rock, but to a group of pebbles. The Crinkled Kelp appears to enjoy this method of attachment and each year as the new blade grows it begins to act as a buoyant sail and it will lift the pebbles clear of the sea bed and float them along in the currents. This is an extraordinary thing to see underwater especially if a whole forest of Crinkled Kelps are on the move. Research by a group of amateur divers has shown that pebble transport by kelp plants can be very important in the build up of shingle banks, which are one of nature's own forms of sea defence. If you find a deep enough rock pool you can try out the kelp sails for yourself; see how well they carry their load of pebbles.

My feet are beginning to get cold and the tide is certainly well on the turn so it's time for me to make my way up the beach and as I do, I am going to collect seaweeds (but only those that have already been broken loose by wave action and cast up on the beach). The small ones go into a polythene bag which has got sea water in the bottom so that they can freshen up. The large kelps, and today I am concentrating on the Rough-stalked one, I will just carry along. There must have been a bad storm recently because there are lots and lots washed up. What I am looking for is one of each size from the smallest to the biggest and I am doing this for a very special reason. . . . Yes, I reckon that I now have enough and all I need is a sandy beach and before your very eyes I will give you a lesson in seaweedology.

There we are, absolutely perfect. You can

Here I am out collecting along the strand line for my 'growth curve' – a nice mixture of Crinkled and Rough-stalked Kelps. In the background you can see the great industrial complex of Teeside.

do this for yourself: draw a straight line in the sand and starting with the smallest kelp lay your collection on the beach with their holdfasts touching the line. Then lay the next biggest and the next, until you have put them all down with the longest ones finally at the right. Now join the tips of each frond up with another line in the sand and what you have got is a perfect growth curve.

What is more, using the technique described earlier you can age each one of the plants and this will mean that you have plotted a 'living graph'. The curve produced by joining the tips of the fronds has a very special name, it is called a sigmoid

A Rough-stalked Kelp with a forest of epiphytic red seaweeds growing along its stipe. Red seaweeds are very difficult to identify but these are mostly *Rhodymenia palmata*.

curve. When young, the plant grows very slowly but after the first couple of years it speeds up into what is called its 'exponential' phase. If you are good at maths you will understand when I say that over that part of the curve the growth of the plant it is undergoing compound interest. If mathematics isn't your strong point then just stand back and admire the kelps' growth curve. Eventually the growth of the older plants slows down as the plant reaches its 'senescent' phase of growth. Eventually it will die, perhaps its buoyant size is just too much for its ageing holdfast, so that it is ripped up by the next storm and we can pick it up on the beach. Remember in nature nothing goes to waste and these rotting seaweeds that make such a nasty smell, provide food for a whole cross-section of creepy crawlies, fungi and bacteria all of which help to break them down eventually leaving the beach clean and healthy.

Before you discard your all-action growth curve take a close look at the holdfasts. As the plant grows, so too does the holdfast and as the latter is made up of all these whorls of branched branches each provides a complex inner space which creates an ideal habitat, a protective home, for a whole range of animals. What is more, as the kelp plant grows so does the volume of the homes in the holdfast. Unfortunately by the time the holdfast has been washed up on the beach all the sensible mobile animals have moved house. However, some will not have been lucky and their remains will be there, still well and truly entangled with the branches.

I went round the world three times to make a series of television programmes about the various major steps in evolution – *Botanic Man*. During that time I met David Attenborough's team doing much the same thing to make his own series, *Life on Earth*. Yet I can guarantee that with a little patience you can see a cross-section of the diversity of the life that we saw on our travels here on the coast, and much of it inside kelp holdfasts. Each of the holdfasts is covered with a felt of mini-plants, single-celled and colonial diatoms, and, in amongst them, are colonies of bacteria. It is this living mini-carpet which helps make the rocks so slippery. There in the largest holdfast, is what looks like a piece of orange rubber, that is a Breadcrumb Sponge, *Halichondria panicea*. It is an aggregate of many millions of cells all working together to produce a very special way of life and certainly it is a lot more complex than the single-celled plants and animals.

Sea anemones are almost everywhere hereabouts. They belong to a group of animals called the Cnidaria which capture their prey by the stinging cells on their tentacles. Here on the kelp is a close relative – a hydroid, a little branched colony looking much more like a plant than an animal. The Cnidaria are simple animals with a sack-like gut; food caught by the tentacles are pushed into the mouth and once digestion is completed inside the body, waste is voided back out through the mouth.

There, poking out of one of the holdfasts, is a lovely green paddle worm. I will lift him, sorry it, they're hermaphrodite, out and put it back in the water where it belongs. This is a much more advanced sort of creature. It is made up of a series of segments and has a one way gut: food goes in at the front and waste goes out at the back – a much more advanced form of creature than the Cnidaria. Another worm, *Spirorbis spirillum*, has built its home on the Crinkled Kelp, this is a little coiled tube shining white and almost translucent against the surface of the kelp. That has probably been washed up from quite deep water and is showing its most characteristic feature: its tube is coiled in an anticlockwise direction. Compare it to the much more abundant homes of *Spirorbis borealis*, whose tube coils in the opposite direction. This is by far the commonest one on the shore and likes to grow on the wracks.

The next group, the molluscs, are virtually everywhere. They are very complex animals and come in a number of basic shapes and forms. There are those with one shell valve, like the winkle over there. Others have two shell valves and by that pool I can see a great knot of mussels which have this feature. The local people used to collect luscious oysters from here before pollution got in the way and those were also bivalve molluscs. The most advanced form of molluscs are the squids and octopuses, but I'm afraid we are unlikely to see one today, although I have seen enormous squid washed up on the shore only a few miles from here. Cuttlefish bones (the white things budgerigars sharpen their beaks on) are not uncommonly washed up on the beach. These are the internal shells of squids and I think that is the nicest thing about the molluscs – when they die of natural causes they leave behind an eminently collectable souvenir, the shell. Well, at least most of them do. So

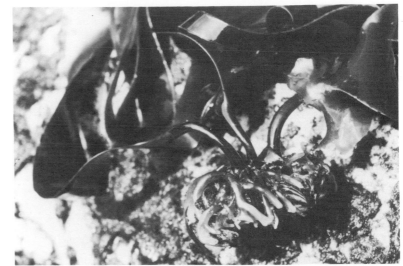

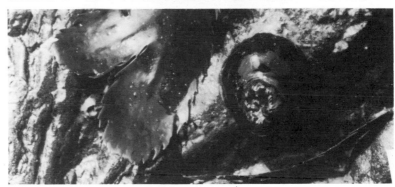

Top **The combined holdfasts of three Smooth-stalked Kelps** (*Laminaria digitata*), **which some mussels had used for safe anchorage.**

Above **Beadlet Anemone** (*Actinia equina*) **with its tentacles retracted – a member of the Cnidaria, the animals with stinging cells. It is lying next to a saw-toothed blade of Serrated Wrack.**

Left **A Green Paddle Worm,** *Eulalia viridis*, **sliding across a rock encrusted with barnacles. This member of the Annelida, segmented worms, is a predator on the barnacles, one of the most numerous animals of our rocky shores.**

Where there is a suitable anchorage on a rock, competition for space is extremely fierce. Therefore you often have several living organisms living on top of each other, all feeding on the feast of plankton brought in at each new tide. Here we have mussels and limpets, members of the Mollusca, encrusted with barnacles, members of the Crustacea, waiting for the sea to cover them.

you never need collect a living mollusc.

Next in the evolutionary ladder comes the animals with jointed legs, the members of the Arthropoda. Lift up a nearby stone and they will come at you from all directions, but remember to put the stone back with care or you might well squash them. Their armour-plated exoskeleton may protect them from their enemies but not from a carelessly placed rock. If I look around in this gully I should be able to find some of their discarded external skeletons. . . . What have I got here? A Shore Crab's nipper and the carapace (upper shell) of a tiny Porcelain Crab. Both of these are just right to put in the marine section of my home museum. What is more, they have been dead and dry for a long time and so won't smell the house out. Now that's not a piece of crab but the arm of an ophiuroid, a brittle-star. This animal belongs to the great group of Spiny-skinned Animals, the Echinodermata. These include the sea urchins, sea cucumbers and sea stars. I will not use the terms starfish, because they are not fish at all.

While on the subject of fish, you have to be quick to see them in the rock pools let alone catch one. Whilst walking across this stretch of beach I have seen several darting for cover under the weeds in the rock pools. They are too quick for me but then, of course, I am a botanist. However, that rapid movement introduces us to the advantage of having a backbone against which muscles can work very efficiently. Next time you eat fish for dinner remember you are eating those power packed muscles which drive the fish through the water with such speed and grace. While thinking about the vertebrates, the animals

with backbones, take a look up and there are several gulls flying over head – a backbone plus warm blood and anything is possible!

Then, of course, there are the mammals. There are plenty further along the beach playing sand castles. This one is half in and half out of a rock pool, but it wouldn't be a rare sight to sit here where I am and see a seal's head bobbing out there in amongst the kelp fronds which are almost submerged. What a morning, I've now got lovely wet feet. We've seen some super plants and seen the whole panoply of evolutionary effort and I didn't have to move much more than a hundred metres. That's why I do like to be beside the seaside.

But now to work. I will now have to write up my notes in my all-important field note-book but unfortunately as usual like most of my things it is now soaking wet. However, I will have to remember to copy it out into my big notebook as soon as I get home. And then also I must deal with all those seaweeds in my plastic bag. When I'm home, I take each specimen out one by one and float them in the sink or a bowl filled with ordinary tap water where they spread themselves out beautifully. I then put a piece of paper under the seaweed (the bond typing paper is best) and lift the paper up very carefully, and with a bit of teasing I find that it has arranged itself on the paper. Next, after I've let it settle down, I lift it out of the water and allow the seaweed to stick itself down on the paper with its own mucilage. Then what I have to do, is to make sure before I press it, that it doesn't stick to the paper I'm going to put on top. Therefore I cover the specimen with a piece of muslin, and then make a newspaper sandwich, remembering to change the newspaper regularly for the first day or so. Meanwhile, I have put my heaviest books on top to press everything down nice and flat and there you are – a perfect specimen. You should then put your piece of paper with its seaweed in your pressed seaweed book. The red seaweeds collected from the strand line can be super to have, and every year I use some of them to make my Christmas cards. In future, if you do get really interested in the seaweeds and learn to identify them, then you should label them and say where, when, and how they were found – and then the seaweeds become a record for the future. Who knows, we could then use your collection in many years to come as valuable evidence for the changes in the sea life around the coast.

HOW TO PRESS YOUR OWN SEA-WEED 1 First float your specimen in a bowl so that the fronds spread out flat; 2 slide a piece of paper carefully under your seaweed and 3 gently place it on some sheets of newspaper, 4 making sure that it is lying flat. 5 You should then lay a sheet of muslin cloth over the seaweed. 6 This protects it from the sheets of newspaper which you place over the top. 7 It is import-ant to replace the newspaper at regular intervals whilst the seaweed is still wet. 8 You should hold the seaweed sandwich down with some of your heaviest books and when it has dried you have a perfect pressed specimen for your seaweed collection.

Coastal Marshes and Estuaries

Estuaries are a magical place. The intermix of fresh and salt water produces a series of environments which are rich in promise. Each day the river brings its own products of erosion, mainly in the form of fine silts, and deposits them along with sands from the sea during periods of slack water. These deposits are full of minerals and are, therefore, rapidly colonised by plants which have evolved to live under the influence of both sweet and salt water. Their roots bind the silt and, in the form of salt marshes, they reclaim the sea, providing pasture for many animals. These rich areas of interconnecting marshes and mudflats are a haven for shorebirds, thousands of which regularly winter along our estuaries and harbours.

Gulls taking off in the evening light from a reed-fringed lagoon at Farlington Marshes.

Information

In Great Britain most of our river estuaries have been shaped by a gradual rise in the sea level, resulting in a gentle gradient where the rivers can deposit the material they have been holding in suspension. Also the sheltered estuary conditions mean that fine material brought in by the tides will also be deposited. The combined effect of these factors produces large areas of mud and sand flats which slope imperceptibly out to sea and which are exposed and covered regularly by the tides. These mudflats are rich in mineral nutrients, therefore the animals that have adapted to the constantly changing salinity and the extremes of weather during exposure are exceptionally numerous. It has been calculated that a square metre of estuarine mud might contain as many as 60000 Laver Spire Shells or a similar number of small crustaceans. These provide food for many thousands of wading birds, such as Dunlins and Oystercatchers, which winter along our coasts. Along the edges of these mudflats saltmarsh plants are able to colonise the higher reaches which are only submerged during spring tides. Gradually by a slow process of accretion and plant succession, the saltmarshes become more permanent, providing homes and feeding areas for many herbivores. Eventually these may be reclaimed by man by the construction of sea walls so that the marsh can be drained to provide permanent pasture for livestock. These reclaimed pastures, if they are not ploughed or treated, are themselves very plant-rich areas and also provide valuable roosting sites for the estuary birds at high tide.

Estuaries therefore, despite their chequered appearance and unpromising acres of mud, can be very rewarding places for a naturalist to visit. But remember do not go marching off across the marshes and mudflats as they can be very treacherous places.

Plant succession on estuarine mudflats

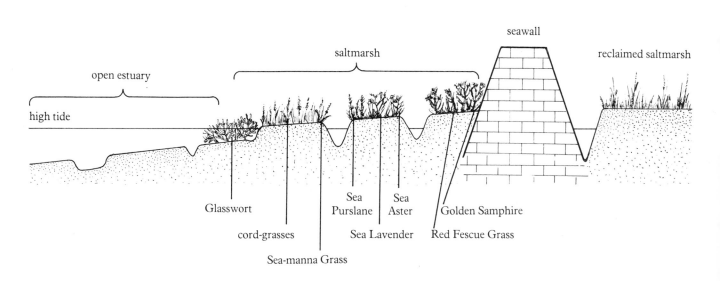

Some plants and animals to look out for:

Plants

Intestine Weed *Enteromorpha intestinalis*
Glasswort *Salicornia europaea*
Sea Lavender *Limonium vulgare*
Sea Puslane *Halimione portulacoides*
Perennial Sea Spurrey *Spergularia media*
Cord Grasses *Spartina* spp.
Sea Aster *Aster tripolium*
Eel Grasses *Zostera* spp.

Invertebrates

Ragworm *Nereis diversicolor*
Tellins *Macoma* spp.
Laver Spire Shell *Hydrobia ulvae*
Cockles *Glycymeris* spp.
Peppery Furrow Shell *Scrobicularia plana*
Sandhopper *Corophium volutator*
Common Shore Crab *Carcinus maenas*

Birds

Brent Goose *Branta bernicla*
White-fronted Goose *Anser albifrons*
Shelduck *Tadorna tadorna*
Pintail *Anas acuta*
Wigeon *Anas penelope*
Teal *Anas crecca*
Oystercatcher *Haematopus ostralegus*
Lapwing *Vanellus vanellus*
Ringed Plover *Charadrius hiaticula*
Grey Plover *Pluvialis squatarola*
Turnstone *Arenaria interpres*
Snipe *Gallinago gallinago*
Curlew *Numenius arquata*
Black-tailed Godwit *Limosa limosa*
Bar-tailed Godwit *Limosa lapponica*
Redshank *Tringa totanus*
Knot *Calidris canutus*
Dunlin *Calidris alpina*
Sanderling *Calidris alba*
Herring Gull *Larus argentatus*
Black-headed Gull *Larus ridibundus*
Common Tern *Sterna hirundo*

Sites

The British Isles is fortunate in having some superb estuaries. The following is a selection from around our coasts. If you are intending to visit any of these it is suggested that you read some of the many regional guides which will tell you the best areas to go to and the places with public access. Always seek local information and permission.

Dornoch Firth, Scottish Highlands. Estuary with extensive saltmarsh. Good birdwatching in autumn and winter.
Cromarty Firth, Scottish Highlands. Large area of sand and mud flats as well as saltmarsh.
Lindisfarne, Northumberland. National Nature Reserve. Interesting area of sand and mud flats. Good birdwatching.
Teeside, Cleveland. Large estuary near industrial conurbation but with some extensive mudflats and saltmarsh. Good birdwatching in winter.
Wash, Lincolnshire/Norfolk. Vast area of estuarine mudflats and saltmarsh of international importance. Good places to visit are Gibraltar Point, Boston Point, Holbeach, Ouse Mouth, Snettisham and Hunstanton.
Walton on the Naze, Essex. Large area of tidal marshes and mudflats. Good winter birdwatching.
North Kent Marshes, Kent. Large area of tidal marshes and mudflats around the Medway and Swale Estuaries, showing all stages of development. Good birdwatching area.
Portsmouth, Langstone, Chichester Harbours, Hampshire/Sussex. Series of inter-tidal inlets with large areas of mudflats, saltmarshes and rough grazing. Good vantage points at Farlington Marshes and Thorney Island. Worth visiting Pagham Harbour along the Sussex coast.
Exe Estuary, Devon. Large areas of mudflats exposed at low tide which provide good birdwatching during the autumn and winter.
Fal Estuary, Cornwall. Series of sheltered inlets with mudflats which provide some interesting birdwatching.
Bridgwater Bay, Somerset. National Nature Reserve. Interesting area with full range of estuary habitats, including sand and mud flats as well as saltmarsh.
Slimbridge, Gloucester. Wildfowl Trust. Good views of high saltmarsh and rough grazing. Excellent for wildfowl in winter. Well worth visiting the Trust's collection.
Dee Estuary, Clwyd/Merseyside. Vast expanses of mudflats and saltmarsh. Large area is a National Wildfowl Refuge. Good birdwatching.
Morecambe Bay, Lancashire/Cumbria. Huge area of inter-tidal sand and mud flats of international importance. Holds probably the largest over-wintering population of waders in Britain.
Caerlaverock, Dumfries. National Nature Reserve. Extensive sand flats and saltmarsh. Visited in winter by large numbers of geese.

Coastal Marshes and Estuaries

with David Billett

For many people the time to visit the coast is during the warm summer months. The idea is probably to search out a sandy beach and have a good splash around, or simply to soak up the sun. Yet, surprisingly enough, there has been an increase in recent years in people visiting the coast, not during the summer, but in the midst of winter. Where are they going and why? Well, most of them are going to the type of coastline that we would drive straight past – mudflats and saltmarsh, swampy looking promontories and wind-swept sea walls. The centre of interest for these intrepid people, wrapped up in their anoraks and welly boots, is the thousands of migratory waders and wildfowl which regularly winter along our coastal marshes and estuaries.

In order to find out why all this was going on in such seemingly inhospitable surrounds, we went down to the South Coast in March to seek out the mud and ooze of Langstone Harbour and, in particular, a reserve called Farlington Marshes which juts out into the

Open estuarine mud-flats and reclaimed saltmarsh. The top photograph shows the exposed mudflats at low tide. Waders and ducks are feeding over them, for although they look rather barren there is a rich harvest of organisms living in the mud. The fertility of the estuarine silts and muds has long been recognised and over the centuries man has reclaimed vast areas of our coast for pasture and arable land. The bottom photograph was taken only metres away from the other and shows clearly the relict gullies and ridges of the saltmarsh in the reclaimed pasture. This grassland has never been ploughed or filled in and is therefore particularly rich in species of grass.

heart of the Harbour. Here we met David Billett, who was to be our guide. He has been studying the wildlife here for over twenty-five years and has seen a lot of changes over this time, including the Marshes new role as a nature reserve. To get the full flavour of a place and really understand what makes it tick, it is important to know something of its history. So before we started out, we asked David to tell us about the origins of the reserve.

'If you take a bird's-eye view of the reserve, you will see that its overall shape is a peninsula. This is largely the result of the reclamation of a series of saltmarsh islands and mudflats in the Eighteenth Century. Some of the reserve, however, includes land that was reclaimed at a much earlier period. The area of pasture near the entrance, for example, is shown as saltmarsh bounded by a sea wall on a map of 1600. In actual fact, reclamation has been going on steadily at least since Roman times. Langstone Harbour and the other large estuaries along this part of the coast are primarily the result of an inundation by the sea in post-glacial times produced by a general rising of the sea level and a lowering of the land − in fact, the south-east of England is slowly sinking into the sea even now!

'The Romans were the first to carry out large scale reclamation. For example, Romney Marsh and the Fens were originally drained under their guidance and many of the foundations for the sea walls of the Thames date originally from this time. In medieval times also, a lot of reclamation was carried out. This time it was at the instigation of the church, who were vast landowners in those days. However, there were great setbacks when falling populations, as a result of tragedies like the Black Death, meant that there was neither the labour, nor the incentive, to reclaim.

'Moving on to more recent times, here, the major part of the land was reclaimed by the Lord of the Manor of Farlington between 1769 and 1773. This fellow appears to have been a fairly enterprising landlord as his neighbours at Bedhampton and Drayton manors left their saltmarsh and mudflats relatively untouched giving us, today, the distinctive peninsular shape of the reserve. From our point of view this has provided us with an ideal mix of habitats − at low tide the waders and wildfowl can feed on the surrounding areas and, during high tide, they use the safety of the reserve as a roost.

'Since the major reclamation the reserve has been used continually as rough grazing for cattle and, today, even though it is managed essentially as a nature reserve, this aspect is still important. If the large areas of pasture were left untouched they would soon become overgrown with long coarse grasses which would not prove as suitable for the birds as the existing grazed land. The Marshes have been managed by the Hampshire and IOW Naturalists' Trust since 1962, currently under a lease from the Portsmouth City Council. This close proximity to the extensive urban areas around Portsmouth has meant that the reserve is important as a recreation area and, in order to minimise disturbance to the wildlife, the Marshes have been divided up into a series of zones with various degrees of access. There are areas in the centre of the reserve which even the wardens rarely visit. This is the main roosting site for the waders and wildfowl. These days, however, the whole of the peninsula could be considered as something of a relict as most of the reclaimed land around the harbour has now been developed. Even here, the north end of the reserve is bordered by a busy motorway.

'Looking out across the reserve we can see that it consists mainly of this rough grazed pasture enclosed by a sea wall. The pasture itself has been discovered to include over a third of the 150 species of grass recorded in Britain. One of the reasons for this incredible diversity is that the pasture over certain parts has never been cultivated. If we walk across into the area with full access we can have a closer look at it.'

We made our way over some bumpy looking ground which was full of apparently dried-up gullies. But then David pointed out the true nature of the land.

'Here we have pasture that is the direct result of the reclamation of saltmarsh. It has been left more or less exactly as it was, so that if you were to cross over to the saltmarsh islands flanking the reserve, you would find the same patterns of gullies and hummocks. This grassland has developed gradually as the salinity of the soil has decreased. It is particularly noticeable here, because there has been no attempt to infill and level-off the ground. If this was unreclaimed there would be salt tolerant plants such as Thrift and Sea Purslane growing on the higher areas, and the channels would be filled with the estuarine muds. Another factor which gives the ground here this uneven appear-

A prickly shroud of Blackthorn, Gorse and Bramble covering the old seawall. This dense thicket of browse-resistant shrubs provides shelter for the visiting birds and is alive with thrushes in the winter, feeding on the fruits.

ance, are the numerous anthills – a good indicator of unimproved grassland.'

We wound our way across the relict gullies towards a slightly higher ridge of land, which was covered with thorny scrub. This was the remains of the old sea wall shown on the 1600 map. It had been found that it was made up of clay and flints with a flint core. There were now large gaps in it, where the sea had breached it over the centuries, before the main sea wall had been constructed. As is often the case when looking for signs of former boundaries and workings, the plants and trees are the main clue to the presence of disturbed soil. Here the wall was covered in

a prickly shroud of Hawthorn, Bramble, Blackthorn and Gorse. The Gorse was very noticeable with its bright yellow flowers. This distant relative of the pea is very quick to take advantage of ground cleared by the workings of man and seems to follow him everywhere. One only has to look at the profusion of Gorse alongside our roads and railways to appreciate that they are still a prolific coloniser. The absence of any Oak trees, which would normally be the climax vegetation of the coastal plain, again was indicative of the goings on of man – the continual use of the area for grazing has meant that only browse resistant shrubs and

trees have managed to establish themselves. Hence the spiny nature of all the plants. The birds, however, love the thick cover that these shrubs have provided and in the winter they are alive with Redwings and Fieldfares from Scandinavia feeding on the succulent fruits.

We then turned away from the old wall with its spiny coat of shrubs, towards the centre of the reserve. But before we moved out to the domain of the winter birds, David had one more surprise up his sleeve. In front of us was an almost circular pond bordered by reeds and to our right could be seen two more similar sized hollows. These, as it

Three ponds filling three bomb craters. Although only separated by some fifty metres they show the effect of differing degrees of salinity. The top one has many interesting freshwater plants and animals such as Broad-leaved Pondweed, frogs and toads. The middle one is slightly saline but still holds some freshwater life. Whilst the third, nearest the sea, is very brackish and has little else living in it other than algae.

turned out, were three craters made by bombs which were originally meant for an anti-aircraft battery sited on the marsh during the Second World War as part of Portsmouth's defences. The way the bombs fell, however, has unwittingly provided a perfect series of examples of the effect of increasing salinity. David takes up the story.

'These bombs did us a good turn because they fell at an angle and the ponds that now fill them indicate very clearly the different salinity to be found on this stretch running down to what was an old tidal creek. Although only separated by some fifty metres and all of approximately the same size the difference between the three ponds is very noticeable.'

We moved on across a stretch of rough grazing towards a reed fringed lagoon, which to most of the visitors must be the heart of the reserve. But before we discussed the bird life we went up onto the sea wall to obtain a better view of the lagoon and the surrounding estuary. The difference between the reclaimed land to our left and the vast areas of mudflats outside the sea wall was quite startling, especially where you could trace the line of the creek on both sides of the wall. We asked David to explain how the present landscape was formed.

'These tidal creeks are often called lakes, and the creek that makes up the lagoon here is called Shut Lake, presumably because at some stage it was cut off from the tide. The level and salinity of the water is now controlled by a simple sluice gate. But before the sea wall was built it would have been possible to navigate a flat-bottomed boat up it for a considerable distance. The land that lies out to sea from here was cut off therefore many years ago and at some time formed two islands, one of which has a very old bank which could possibly be an old Iron Age stock compound. In fact, there is a lot of evidence that these islands are the eroded higher remnants of land submerged at a much earlier period. There is evidence from the dense scatter of prehistoric flint tools and pottery, which occurs across the whole area, that during these earlier times it was much used for hunting, fishing and grazing.'

It was interesting to reflect that even here, on what looks like a last remnant of former wilderness, man had made his indelible stamp. David pointed out that it was safe to say that really, apart from a few cliffs and mountain tops there is really nowhere in Britain that has not been affected by man.

Two views of the same creek. The photograph below shows the creek running out across the mudflats, with the base of the seawall and the sluice gate in the foreground. The photograph on the opposite page shows the creek on the landward side of the wall. The fringing reedbeds add an important dimension to this habitat, providing shelter and a source of food throughout the year. One of the first management projects on the reserve was to fence off the lagoon so that the reeds could develop without grazing pressure.

'The success today of the reserve as a "natural habitat" for birds is also a question of careful management by man. A good example, is the way that Shut Lake has developed. One of the first things we did, when we took over the management of the reserve, was to build a fence along the entire length of the lagoon, which isolated the area from any grazing, and allowed the reeds to grow back from the lagoon edge. This has now produced a fairly extensive reed bed, which for this part of the coast, adds an interesting dimension to the habitat. A reed bed like this, apart from providing year round protection and shelter for the wild-fowl, has its own fauna. For example, the Harvest Mouse breeds in here. They make a nest which is about the size of a cricket ball, made of carefully woven reeds and grass stems. The nest is very elastic and grows in size with the developing mice. The Harvest Mouse is a fantastic animal to watch as it is very acrobatic, swinging around like a little monkey with its prehensile tail. Another speciality of coastal reed beds is the Bearded Tit which started coming here in the mid-sixties. From ringed birds we discovered that they were commuting every winter from the extensive reed beds on the east coast, such as at Minsmere and Walberswick, in Suffolk. These days we tend to get them mainly on passage. They can be very conspicuous when they are here, if you get a calm day. You usually hear them first, with their distinctive call which is rather like a banjo-string being plucked.'

We scanned the open water of the lagoon for ducks. A few Shelducks were feeding on the far side and little groups of Teal and Mallard were either quietly resting or foraging around on the fringes for food. When we had come here earlier in the year the water was thick with birds but at the moment it was comparatively quiet. David pointed out that this was partly because it was low tide and a lot of the ducks were out feeding on the saltmarshes. But essentially this was a place to go to in the coldness of winter or during the autumn. We asked David what sort of birds could be found here at various times during the year.

'As you can see there are not too many ducks here at the moment. There are still a few Mallard and Teal. During the winter we have the surface ducks on the lagoon – Shoveler, Pintail, Teal, Mallard and some Wigeon. The Wigeon are more wary than the others and prefer to be on the mudflats

or, if they come in at high tide, they like to be on the pasture land in the centre of the reserve, where they can feed on the grass and remain secluded. Teal are the commonest duck on the lagoon in winter; you can see several hundred here at times. The Shoveler numbers can go up to a hundred. As their name suggests, they have large shovel-like bills through which they filter their food. The Pintail are wary, like the Wigeon, but they do seem to like coming in on the freshwater that the lagoon provides at high tide. In general the numbers of wildfowl have increased. On the reserve this is entirely due to the management. But interestingly numbers nationally have increased as well. There have been far more Wigeon, Teal, Pintail and Shoveler coming into England since the mid-sixties. Nobody seems to be quite sure what this is due to, but it has probably something to do with two main factors. One is the increasing provision for wildfowl refuges, for example at Slimbridge and the Ouse Washes, and a more discriminating approach to shooting from the wildfowlers. Another factor is that the Dutch reclamation schemes have reached a stage where they do not provide so much open water in winter. The numbers of Wigeon coming here seem to support this idea. Whereas at one time, our peak numbers of Wigeon used to be reached during the periods of hard weather in the winter, we now get a peak at the end of October or early November; we get this great passage through the area and then numbers level off towards mid-winter. These are birds which we think would have stayed in Holland until they were frozen out. But with the vast amount of reclamation that has gone on in recent years a lot of places that would have held them have been lost. So, ironically places like Farlington have benefited from the Dutch activities. But it is important to reflect that if attitudes here were different, the wildfowl would have been further restricted.

'If you look back to the fifties, when there was no conservation management here, the place was shot over all winter and very often the rest of the year as well. As a result very few waders or wildfowl came in onto the pasture at high tide. Wildfowl only ever came in at dusk and the Wigeon came in later under cover of darkness. But even then they were immediately shot at and flew straight out again. So they had no confidence in coming in here at all. However, as soon as

October on Shut Lake with a good variety of ducks and waders. How many different species can you identify?

Mallard, Teal, Pintail, Shoveler, Moorhen, Lapwing, Snipe, Dunlin, Herring Gull and more!

we stopped the shooting and started to provide security for them, they responded by coming here in considerable numbers. With wildfowl you can show rapid results and within the first winter of controlling the shooting the numbers using the reserve had increased noticeably. Since then the wildfowl have been very much a feature of the place in winter. It is now possible to see anything up to 500 or 600 Wigeon grazing by this lagoon and the flood flashes on the centre of the reserve. Teal reach the same kind of numbers on the reserve as well. We have even larger numbers of Brent Geese, which can now reach over 7000.'

I put it to David that, therefore, areas like this are now becoming increasingly important on an international scale as winter habitats for these wildfowl and waders.

'This harbour with Chichester harbour next door are extremely important, because on the south coast of England they constitute the largest area of inter-tidal habitat. A lot of mudflats are unfortunately not as rich in invertebrate fauna as we have here. If you compare this with Poole Harbour, which looks very similar on a map, Poole is much poorer in the numbers of surface ducks and waders, because the surrounding land is very acid heathland, which means the alluvial silt being deposited in the harbour is not as productive as here. Poole has a lot of diving duck but these are fishing for fry or small fish which are coming in from the sea. The mudflats around here are vast – to give you some idea of the size, Langstone Harbour contains something like 15000 acres. It is about four miles from the northern shore to the harbour mouth and about three and a half miles from east to west, which, all in all, is quite a lot of square mileage of alluvial mudland, saltmarsh, shingle beach and low mud cliffs. The southern aspect and the waters draining off the chalk downland behind all combine to increase the productivity of the harbour.'

We looked out across the expanse of mudflats which were intersected with little winding creeks and patches of saltmarsh. A group of wading birds took flight about 70 metres away. Twisting and turning, they showed their silvery white coloration and black axillaries, which we could make out through the binoculars, indicated that they were Grey Plovers which were probably resting before continuing their journey to the high Arctic to breed. To most people these acres of ooze must seem a vast wet waste of space, completely devoid of life. Was this a valid point of view? I asked David.

'Those mudflats are probably the most highly productive form of habitat you can find. More productive than the equivalent amount of agricultural land. If it was reclaimed it would, of course, be highly productive as farm land. But, as it stands, most of the things that live on it we would not want to eat. Although the harbour has supported oyster beds – which at one time were probably the most important industry in the harbour. However, if you look at it from the point of view of it producing life alone, the amount of animal and plant life, which is dependent on it, is fantastic. This area in winter has between twenty and thirty thousand Dunlin working over it. On top of that you have perhaps 1000 Bar-tailed Godwits, 1000 Grey Plovers, over 1000 Curlews, plus countless thousands of gulls, and, of course, the Shelducks, Brent Geese and other wildfowl.'

The Brent Geese were obviously a speciality of the area and I asked David to tell us some more about these evocative birds.

'The main food of the dark-bellied race of the Brent Geese used to be the eel grasses (*Zostera*). One of the types of these grass was a principal food of the Brent Goose and unfortunately it started to die back throughout the goose's range, until in the twenties and thirties it had almost become extinct. Since then, however, it has made a rapid recovery and is now becoming quite common on the mudflats. Meanwhile the Brent, which had allegedly suffered because of the lack of this food, had diminished quite markedly in numbers. Counts made after the Second World War put their total world population at between 10000 and 15000. Now they have built up to well over 100000 and the increase may well continue. This recovery was due, in part, to the fact that the Brent was forced to find other sources of food and they turned to the more plentiful marine algae. This green stuff, which is carpeting the flats here in front of us, is a marine algae called *Enteromorpha*, and is one of their main foods now. It is, however, not as nutritious as the eel grass, and so they have to eat a lot more to keep going. They have existed on this for quite a long time but are now changing their habits yet again. They are now starting to come in to feed on pasture, like the grey geese – a thing which was unheard of until recently. This change of direction seems to have given them an even greater boost because we are finding that the Marshes are supporting far larger numbers of geese than they would have done twenty years ago.

'In the early fifties it was exciting to see a hundred geese at a distance. Now it is possible to walk up to within 20 or 30 metres of them. There have been some here this winter, where you could get so close that you could read the numbers on their rings with the naked eye. This new feeding habit of moving in onto pasture land has also meant that, when they have flocked on land with winter cereals, they have quickly become unpopular with the coastal farmers.

'Apart from the changes in their feeding strategies and the protection from shooting that they now have through most of western Europe, their numbers have also been helped by the reserves that the Russians have set up in their breeding grounds. Formerly, the local inhabitants used to feed on the geese, particularly in late summer when the birds were beginning to migrate – the young birds would begin this on foot as their flight feathers were not fully developed, making them easy prey to round up and catch.'

Most of the geese had flown but a reluctant flock was still feeding out on the pasture in the centre of the reserve. There seemed to be a lot of head bobbing and squabbling going on, as the pair bonds were being established. It is important that the courtship rituals are begun whilst they are still in their winter quarters, in order that the business of egg laying and rearing the young can be started as soon as they arrive in their breeding grounds during the short arctic summer. It seemed strange to think that soon they would be many hundreds of miles away in the Siberian wastes, as here they were busy feeding against an all too British backdrop of motorways and red-brick housing estates.

The opportunistic approach that the Brent Geese appear to have taken to their feeding habits seemed to reflect the changing fortunes of the vegetation of the Harbour, as I found out from David.

'This *Enteromorpha*, which the Brent Geese feed on, will often spread right across these flats. It seems to have increased very rapidly in the last ten years or so. There seems to be some indication that this is related to the increased nitrogen inflow into these harbours from the various sewage works around. There is also evidence to indicate that the increased use of chemical fertilizers on neighbouring agricultural land is also having some effect, through run-off into ditches and the harbour. Although this increase is good for the Brent, it does have a blanketing effect on the mudlands. In the summer you can find vast sheets of the *Enteromorpha* around here. Underneath it the invertebrate fauna, which is normally very dense, suffers badly from the lack of light. Whether this has any long term effect we just do not know. Obviously some waders cannot probe through it. Short-billed waders probably find it difficult to find food where there is an extensive covering. On the other hand autumn gales very often rip it all up and blow it off quickly. Fortunately this is when the majority of the waders start arriving and searching for food.

'The only obvious change in bird populations that might be related to this is in the numbers of Shelduck, which have decreased dramatically in the last twenty years. We used to expect 3000 to 4000 Shelduck to winter here. Today they very seldom go over a 1000, with 1500 at the very most. There may be other reasons for this decline. For example, it may be that a long succession of mild winters have meant that the ducks have not been forced down to the South Coast as they have done during former hard winters, and that numbers in other parts of the country have gone up. The Thames Estuary, since it has become cleaner, has now more Shelduck. If you go to the North East, Teesmouth now has large numbers wintering there. Another factor could be simply the very high numbers of Brent Geese which now go up to about 7000 – this

Brent Geese, *Branta bernicla*, **flying in from the saltmarsh to feed on the rough pastures of Farlington during high tide.**

Above *Hydrobia*,
molluscs which feed
on the rotting
Enteromorpha. These
tiny animals are a rich
source of food for the
Shelducks on the
mudflats and salt-
marsh.

Opposite top **The
foundations of a once
large house can still
be seen along the
shore. A final
reminder of the once
extensive oyster
fisheries that were an
important industry in
the harbour.**

**A flint scraper found
on the saltmarsh.
These ancient imple-
ments indicate that
the coastal areas have
always been important
to man.**

winter we reached our largest number ever
in November with 7 500. It could be that
there is simply not the elbow room in the
harbour for two large wildfowl. However,
they certainly do not compete for food, as
the Shelduck feed almost entirely on a tiny
mollusc called *Hydrobia*, which from a
distance looks like fine shingle. The *Hydrobia*
feed on vegetation and bacteria so they
should do well on rotting *Enteromorpha*.
Obviously there needs to be some careful
research over a period of time before we can
really be sure of the reasons for the trends
we are seeing.'

Further around the reserve towards the
headland we came to a patch of saltmarsh
that was just beside the seawall. David
suggested that we go down and have a look
at it. We clambered down the new concrete
face of the seawall and on to some short,
spiny looking grass. We had a closer look at
this tough looking plant while David related
the story of its arrival on our coasts.

'This is *Spartina*, cord grass. It is, in fact,
a hybrid race which originated in South-
ampton Water, when an American species
Spartina alterniflora, which some say they
used as a packing in the ships in the same
way as hay, was thrown overboard and
fragments rooted down. This new coloniser
hybridized with the British *Spartina maritima* to form a very vigorous hybrid,
Spartina × townsendii. This plant not only
proved to be extremely vigorous but also
proved to be genetically very interesting.
Normally hybrids have to propagate themselves vegetatively as they are sterile, but
this hybrid cord grass was able to set seed
and therefore acted like a new species. This
invasion originally happened in the late
Nineteenth Century and, for many years, it

spread everywhere progressively taking over
our coastline. A lot of people thought it was
going to be the reclamationist's dream, as it
thrived on bare mudflats and vast areas of
the coast were planted with it. But recently
it has started to die back in areas, as it builds
up a silt layer and after a while this silt layer
becomes so thick that it suffocates the plant.
Of course, where it has died back, the mud-
flat that it had reclaimed is being swept
away. I have a photograph, taken fifteen
years ago, which shows the *Spartina* hybrid
growing all around the Marshes. Now there
is very little here at all.'

We moved a bit further out on to a small
bank of saltmarsh. To my surprise David
pointed out that on the 1600 map this area
is shown as having a house with a garden
and a paddock attached. Apparently there
had been a house standing there up until
1820. The person living there was probably
looking after the oyster fisheries. Now there
was no apparent sign of any former human
habitation. Even the plant life was only just
managing to survive. On top of the bank
was the first spring growth of some typical
saltmarsh plants – Sea Lavender, Sea
Purslane and Sea Beet. The leaves formed
tight rosettes low on the surface and looked
very like succulents. Although the plants are
growing with one 'foot' in the sea, they
cannot make use of the highly saline water
held in the saltmarsh soils and must be
adapted to conserve water, hence their
succulence and leathery, almost cacti-like,
appearance.

David pointed out that it was sometimes
possible to discover pieces of prehistoric
pottery and various flint implements out on
the saltmarsh, especially along the edges of
the marsh which were being constantly
eroded, washing out various artefacts. His
trained eye eventually alighted on a small
piece of reddish stone.

'This is something which has just worked

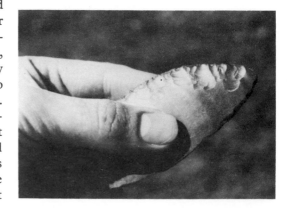

its way down through the brickearth to a level where the underlying London Clay forms a barrier.'

We had a close look at it and could see that it was made of clay. The surface was flecked with small bits of flint.

'You see that ground-up flint incorporated in the clay, this is to stop it cracking when it is fired. This is probably a piece of pot, possibly Bronze Age. This bit is probably from one of those big storage jars, sometimes you can actually find them with their original finger prints.'

It was the last place I would have expected to find such things. David pointed out that trained archaeologists can learn a tremendous amount from these fragments and any pieces that are found should be sent to the local museum. We headed on back along the sea wall towards the end of the peninsula. On the landward side, we passed along the main roosting area and then moved across a strip of land which was much more overgrown than the grazed areas.

'This is a zone that we do not graze in the hope that it will eventually 'scrub up', making it more suitable in winter for birds like the Short-eared Owl. The longer grass

will make it more attractive to voles, which the owls feed on. These small rodents like to tunnel in the rank grasses, making honeycomb-like runs everywhere.'

We climbed back onto the sea wall and surveyed the huge expanse of mudflats in front of us. A few Redshanks were calling noisily and a group of Oystercatchers was feeding on the far shore. Little flocks of Dunlin were skirting around the headland like low wisps of smoke. Ringing studies carried out on these little waders have shown

Waders and Little Terns roosting in the Exe Estuary. This early spring gathering has some birds already in their breeding plumage. The large waders at the back are Bar-tailed Godwits and Oystercatchers with Grey Plovers and Dunlins in the foreground.

A Short-eared Owl quartering the pasture at Farlington in search of voles. Unlike many of our owls, these spectacular birds can often be seen flying during daylight hours.

always thought to be a relatively plentiful farmland bird.

'The Lapwing is rapidly becoming a species in need of conservation. At one time it was a common bird on farmland and heathland, as well as coastal marshes like this. In the south-east of England it is becoming very much scarcer and, unfortunately, like so many of these things, it is difficult to know exactly what this is due to. Here, at Farlington its numbers fluctuate widely, sometimes we can have as many as fifty pairs breeding, which is a very high density for the species. At other times it drops right down to less than twenty pairs. Hard winters have an effect as they drive the birds out of the area. The Lapwing responds very quickly to changes in temperature – as soon as there is an approaching spell of cold weather they are off across the channel, or into Ireland. Certainly, here we find that numbers are much reduced in spring after a hard winter. Another factor is that Lapwings need certain conditions to nest. For example, they will not nest in long grass, they like to be able to see all around and also the chicks need to have a short, relatively dry sward to run about in, with areas of water nearby so that, if it becomes too dry, they can go off and find food around the edges of the ditches or ponds. They are a bird which, like the Skylark, needs a short tussocky rough pasture, but they do not like artificial pasture. They will breed, though in spring cereals. However, then the trouble is that the crop grows so rapidly that, by the time the young are hatched, the cereals are too tall and when they are treated and rolled the Lapwing can be really finished off. This is one of the reasons why they have gone

that they are part of a population which breeds in Siberia. They have a distinct migration route through the Baltic and along the coast of the Low Countries, they then moult either in Holland or the Wash in September and October before dispersing to other areas in this country, including Langstone Harbour. Some of the Turnstone, Redshank and Black-tailed Godwits have proved to have come from Iceland, and in the case of Knot, even from Greenland. But Farlington is now also becoming increasingly important in providing breeding habitats for some of our waders. The loud, distinctive call of the Redshank had been with us all day and we could see the displaying males skittering across the fields. Some Lapwing were also moving about on the reserve centre. These two birds have both suffered from recent changes in land use and are now becoming uncommon in lowland Britain. As the noisy waders got on with their courtship rituals I asked David to tell us more about the Lapwing, which I had

A Lapwing feeding amongst some Brackish Water Crowfoot. This farmland bird has suffered from agricultural improvements and is now rapidly disappearing as a breeding species from large areas of lowland Britain.

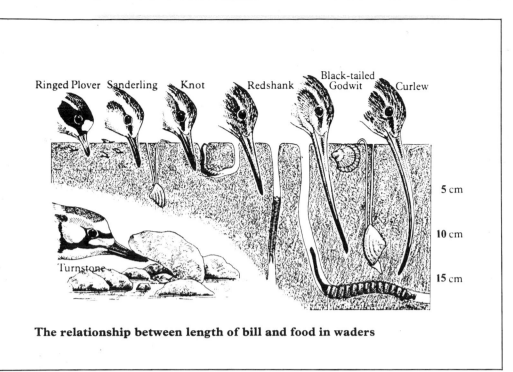

Ringed Plover Sanderling Knot Redshank Black-tailed Godwit Curlew

Turnstone

5 cm

10 cm

15 cm

The relationship between length of bill and food in waders

from so much arable farmland. But we do not know why they are also decreasing on suitable sites.

'Organisations like the RSPB are taking an increasing interest in the flood meadows which have suitable stretches for breeding Lapwings and other birds such as Redshank and Yellow Wagtail. Because of the specific breeding requirements for birds such as these, it is vitally important that the pasture on the reserve here is grazed correctly. We aim to have a short sward all the year round, which means that we need to have hard grazing during the autumn and fairly light herds grazing during the early spring.

The optimum stocking rate would seem to be one animal per acre. Above that we tend to get looooo, particularly with the Lapwing, through trampling. However, Lapwing will defend a nest and young very actively and continue to sit hard even if the cattle are grazing right up against them. When the cattle get too close they will get up and threaten them, usually the cattle then stop and have a look at what is going on, then move off. I have seen horses actually nuzzle right into a nest and, I suspect, eat the eggs.'

By now we had walked around most of the reserve. The tide was beginning to turn and soon the great creeks with their banks of mudflats would be covered over. A small group of Yellow Wagtails heralding the coming spring with their sulphur yellow underparts were darting about on some open ground near the sea wall. Hopefully a successful breeding season was on the way for the Lapwings and Redshank. A small flock of Bar-tailed Godwits had taken up residence on the roosting area of the reserve, some were showing the bright chestnut of their breeding plumage. Soon they would be off, like the Grey Plovers, to the High Arctic to breed, before returning to these superb feeding grounds.

What had been so striking, as we had walked around the reserve was how important it was to maintain the diversity of habitats and provide somewhere where the birds could be secure. After all, they have been wintering along these coastal marshes and estuaries for longer than there have been human settlements here. It is the very least we can do to provide them with a place to feed and rest. Fortunately, more people are becoming aware of their presence, and are discovering the strange romance that these places have – perhaps, it is the thrilling sight of thousands of Dunlin reeling above the surface of the water, or the haunting cries of the Curlew. Perhaps, it is the chance of seeing a rare visitor foraging amongst the droves of feeding wildfowl or roosting gulls. Let us hope that such places will continue to be looked after under the capable supervision of organisations like the Hampshire and IOW Naturalists' Trust, so that future generations can experience these wonderful sights and sounds.

Sea Cliffs

When man first arrived in Britain, the vast majority of our landscapes were covered with dense forest. There were, however, a few places that remained open, such as the edges of lakes and rivers and, in particular, the sea cliffs with their unstable rocky surfaces beaten by salt laden winds. Uncluttered by tall vegetation these areas are of special importance and interest, for not only do they provide superb vistas over the surrounding coastline but they also allow you to see the underlying rock types and the way these affect the surface vegetation.

Mary Gillham has an immense knowledge of the whole world of botany. Here, in a walk along part of the South Wales coast she describes some of the typical plants and animals to be found.

A sweeping view along the Glamorgan coast. Cliff top walks can be very exhilarating with their tremendous landscapes and fascinating plants and animals.

Cliff Formation

Cliffs are formed by the destructive action of the waves as they pound against our rocky coasts. Not only does the sea water itself hit the rock face with tremendous force but a high pressure spray is driven into every nook and cranny, compressing the air trapped in the crevices. As the wave recedes this air expands suddenly, often loosening quite large rocks. This relentless bombarding of the rocks eventually breaks up the surface, particularly where there are already weaknesses such as fault lines. Gradually the cliff face is eroded back by a series of minor falls or occasionally whole sections topple into the sea leaving the exposures of bare rock that we term cliffs. These cliffs tell us a great deal about the nature of the underlying rock. Where it is horizontally bedded the cliff face tends to be almost sheer, particularly where the rock is porous as in chalk or limestone, as there is little surface run-off from water at the head of the cliff. Where the rock is soft they tend to be prone to subsidence in the form of extensive landslips which means that the cliff profile is much more rounded. As the cliffs are eroded back by the waves, the rock surface below the mean sea-level, which is subjected to much less erosion, forms a platform over which the fallen rocks from the cliff can be found. This area can provide a fascinating habitat for the animals and plants of the littoral zone. But remember, it is dangerous to walk beneath the cliffs as they are highly unstable.

The higher areas of the cliff face provide an important ecological niche. Land plants that are unable to compete with some of the more dominant plants can be found here. These ledges also provide a site for plants away from the grazing pressures of sheep and rabbits. Cliffs in spring can be alive with the sound of nesting seabirds which also take advantage of their inaccessibility to get away from predatory mammals.

Zonation of breeding birds on a sea cliff

Some plants and birds to look out for:
Some cliff nesting birds

Fulmar *Fulmarus glacialis*
Gannet *Sula bassana*
Cormorant *Phalacrocorax carbo*
Shag *Phalacrocorax aristotelis*
Herring Gull *Larus argentatus*
Kittiwake *Rissa tridactyla*
Razorbill *Alca torda*
Guillemot *Uria aalge*
Black Guillemot *Cepphus grylle*
Puffin *Fratercula arctica*
Rock Dove *Columba livia*
Raven *Corvus corax*
Jackdaw *Corvus monedula*
Chough *Pyrrhocorax pyrrhocorax*
Rock Pipit *Anthus spinoletta*

Cliff erosion

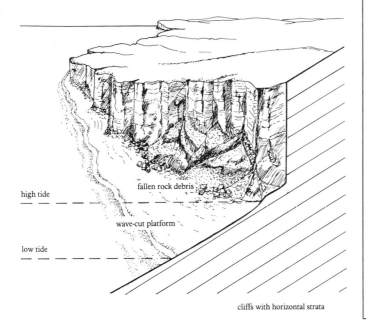

high tide

fallen rock debris

wave-cut platform

low tide

cliffs with horizontal strata

Plants

Lichens – the bases of the cliffs are often zoned with distinctive yellow and black lichens:

Xanthoria parietina (yellow)
Ramalina siliquosa (grey)
Verrucaria maura (black)

Flowering plants – the cliff tops are frequently starred with dwarf forms of grassland species

Thrift *Armeria maritima*
Rock Sea Lavender *Limonium binervosum*
Samphire *Crithmum maritinum*
Scottish Lovage *Ligusticum scoticum*
Common Scurvy Grass *Cochlearia officinalis*
Wild Cabbage *Brassica oleracea*
Wild Carrot *Daucus carota*
Sea Storksbill *Erodium maritimum*
Rock Sea-spurrey *Spergularia rupicola*
Sea Pearlwort *Sagina maritima*
Sea Campion *Silene maritima*
Yellow Stonecrop *Sedum acre*
Vernal Squill *Scilla verna*

Sites

The following is a selection of cliff walks around our coasts. Some of the offshore islands are only accessible at certain times and it is suggested that you consult some of the many regional guides before intending to visit any of the sites. Remember cliffs can be dangerous places.

Westray, Orkneys. One of the northern islands in the Orkneys with excellent cliffs and large seabird colonies.
Hoy, Orkneys. The most westerly island in the Orkneys with extensive cliffs and the famous Old Man of Hoy. Large seabird colonies.
Bass Rock, Lothian. Regular boat trips are run around this isolated rock in summer which is famous for its Gannet colony.
St Abbs Head, Borders. Eight miles of cliffs which reach over 150 metres (500 feet) in height. Seabird colonies. Scottish Wildlife Trust reserve.
Farne Islands, Northumberland. Group of islands belonging to the National Trust. Full range of coastal habitats including cliffs with large seabird colonies.
Flamborough Head and Bempton Cliffs, Humberside. Spectacular chalk cliffs rising to 140 metres (450 feet) with large colonies of seabirds. Bempton Cliffs is an RSPB reserve.
Beachy Head, Sussex. Famous chalk cliffs rising to 160 metres (500 feet). Nature Trails.
The Needles, Isle of Wight. Chalk cliffs owned by the National Trust. Seabirds and magnificent views.
Purbeck Cliffs, Dorset. Spectacular stretch of limestone cliffs with interesting flora and good seabird colonies.

Lulworth Cove, Dorset. Famous beauty spot with three-mile coastal walk from Lulworth to Durdle Dor.
Cornwall Coast Path. Cornwall has some magnificent stretches of cliffs, anyone planning to explore the area should consult the *Cornwall Coast Path* by E. C. Pyatt. HMSO.
Dunraven, Glamorgan. Excellent stretch of limestone cliffs designated as 'Heritage Coastline' (see page 50).
Gower Peninsula, Glamorgan. Good cliff walks at Mumbles Head and Port Eynon. Seabird colonies at Worms Head; National Nature Reserve.
Pembroke Coast Path, Dyfed. The coast between Cardigan and Tenby has some superb stretches of cliffs with interesting offshore islands, notably Skomer Island. Anyone wishing to explore this coast should consult *The Pembroke Coast Path* by John Barrett. HMSO.
South Stack, Holy Island, Gwynedd. Cliffs teeming with seabirds during the spring and early summer. Open May to mid-July.
St Bees Head, Cumbria. Magnificent Red Sandstone Cliffs with large seabird colonies.
Mull of Galloway, Galloway. Interesting area of cliffs with seabirds. Southern most point of Scotland.
Outer Hebrides, Western Isles. Some spectacular areas of cliffs, particularly on some of the smaller islands. Before planning to visit it is best to look fully in to access.
Dunnet Head, Highland. A superb remote cliff with extensive seabird colonies.

Sea Cliffs
with
Mary Gillham

When you are at the seaside one of the most relaxing pursuits is to get away from the bustle of a crowded beach and take a gentle stroll along one of the many cliff paths along our coast. Quite often, the aim of the walk is simply to reach that bit further along the coast and find a secluded beach away from the main car park or seaside town. Whatever the motive, these cliff walks cross some very interesting stretches of grassland, and always provide splendid views. You can often find yourself wondering what on earth all the flowers are, or admiring the butterflies busily flying from one bloom to the next, or just watching the great waves crashing against the cliffs. Well, next time you are on one of these gentle strolls, stop and have a closer look. You will be amazed at the diversity of plants and animals that live along our cliffs.

We went for just such a walk at Dunraven in South Wales with Dr Mary Gillham who, apart from having studied coastal plants around the world, is also an author and the Chairman of the Glamorgan Naturalists' Trust. We arrived at the coast on a blustery June morning, and having made sure we had packed our lunches, we set off towards the headland called Trwyn-y-witch, the Witch's Nose. While we were still down by the beach, Mary introduced us to the overall geography of the site.

'Here we are on the Glamorgan coast, about half-way between Cardiff and Swansea. West of here, right to Swansea we have a tremendous sweep of sand interrupted by rocks only at Porthcawl. Beyond that there is the marvellous old limestone cliffs of the Gower peninsula. To the east, we have cliffs of newer liassic limestone, and 14 miles of these have recently been designated as "Heritage Coastline". This is now one of fourteen areas around the coast of Britain which are designated for amenity and conservation purposes. Further east again are cliffs of red Triassic rocks, merging into mudflats along the north side of the Severn Estuary above Cardiff. Although well down the Bristol Channel, Dunraven experiences some of its enormous tides, which are the second biggest in the world, over 12 metres (40 feet) during spring tides. There is probably about a 10 metre (30 feet) rise and fall here today. At the start of our walk there is a magnificent sandy beach, stretching out a fifth of a mile to the headland, and across the water we can just make out the hills of Exmoor.

'Running inland from the beach is quite a broad valley, but there is no river in the bottom of it. This is rather like the dry valleys of the English chalklands. The rock is a very porous limestone which means that the water seeps through to run underground and emerge as springs out at sea. In peri-glacial times, however, when the ice was melting, the sub-soil was frozen as a layer of perma-frost which the water could not drain through. Instead it flowed over the surface, carving the valley which subsequently "dried out". The water of that ancient river cut down through the cliffs and through the rocky beach platform as well. The ensuing gap then sanded over to give us today's broad bay. The beach sand is quite exposed and gets churned around by the waves which come pounding in from the south west. Its lovely yellow colour

shows that there is little organic material in it to feed shellfish, worms and sandhoppers, so you are unlikely to find many wading birds looking for food here.

'There is another side valley which does have a stream running on the surface, but only for about a quarter of a mile. The water surfaces part-way up the valley from a series of underground springs. Again it is rather like one of the chalk streams on the Downs of Southern England, with its fine sediments of limey mud. It is well worth looking at, because it is teeming with animal life: shrimps, caddis larvae and water snails.

We walked up beside this stream behind the headland. It was garlanded with a profusion of plants from Water Crowfoot and Fool's Watercress to Water Mint and various grasses such as Marsh Foxtail and Flotegrass. We crossed over a footbridge above

which there was only a tiny trickle of a stream, but the extent of the bordering marsh was indicated by stands of Yellow Flag, Meadowsweet and the ubiquitous Hard Rush.

As we climbed the slope above the stream towards the headland we looked back towards the main dry valley and noticed the effect of the prevailing south-westerly winds on the vegetation. Mary described the scene.

'Back down in the dry valley at the end nearest the sea, the scrub looks solid enough to walk on. It is bevelled gently down to ground level on the windward flank, providing marvellous cover for small animals such as Rabbits. In places, the wind funnelling up the valley has broken through this armoury of tightly packed branches and bitten back deeply into the wood. There you

Above **A male Stone-chat perched on a song post. Its call sounds like two stones being struck together, hence its name.**

Opposite top **A Hawthorn almost bent double by the wind. The direction of its main growth shows that the prevailing wind direction is from the south-west.**

can see that all the seaward Sycamore trees are dead or on their last legs. Interestingly, despite this there is still enough humidity at ground level for ferns to grow, and these are mostly Hart's Tongue and Male Ferns. The Gorse clumps on the nearer exposed slope are also wind smoothed, and during gales the windward side of the bushes become "browned-off" and dead, with practically all the growth on the leeward side. This means that the bushes appear to be crawling gently uphill. During calmer spells hardy pioneer plants will start to grow again to windward, so in the long term the community remains reasonably stable.

'Looking at another wood further inland, we can see more trees killed by wind. A few years ago there were gales in May which killed almost all the leaves for several miles inland, so that it looked just like autumn, although it was still spring. Only those trees which came into leaf late in the year remained unscathed. So although some of these trees may be over 60 metres above sea level, the effect of salt-laden winds can still be devastating. It is also worth looking at some of the large dead trunks that are lying on the leeward of the hill and supplying sustenance for innumerable fungi and small animals. They are the remains of a beech

wood that was planted during the Nineteenth Century. The trees are all dead now, but there must have been a long calm spell in the latter part of the century for them to have been able to grow to full size.

'Some of the wind-battered scrub here is used by the Stonechats as song posts. These delightful birds share these exposed grassy headlands by the sea with Linnets and Wheatears, but they need some kind of eminence to get up on and sing, to tell the chap next door to please keep to his own patch. The dead trees are riddled with beetle holes and are full of living titbits for the woodpeckers. You are quite likely to hear the laughing call of a Green Woodpecker as you go up the slope. The butterfly, which seems to enjoy the wind more than the others here, is the Red Admiral and you can encounter it up on the headland battling with the breeze and find yourself wondering how its frail body can cope.

'To our right, by the edge of the cliff, you can see a series of ridges and furrows. These are the remnants of an Iron Age promontory fort which was built on the site of an older Mesolithic encampment. These Iron Age forts are quite a feature of our coasts and are usually found, like this one, on headlands overlooking bays which were good landing places. Some of the forts were probably occupied up to the time of the Roman invasion. Because these cliffs are so erodible, the sea is breaking them away all the time, and as much as half of this particular fort has now disappeared into the sea, so that instead of being circular, it is now more or less semi-circular. If you look at it from down on the beach, you will be able to see a cross-section of the man-made banks and make out sea-rounded pebbles and beach boulders which some poor chap either had to carry up on his back from the beach below or haul up the cliff face in baskets. Archaeologists have found a core of turf in the middle of some of these mounds, presumably material that was dug out of the ditch alongside. If you look carefully, you will find that some of the original mounds have smaller ones superimposed upon them. These are more modern, being medieval "pillow mounds", which functioned as Rabbit warrens. They are simply mounds of earth which the Rabbits were able to burrow into. Rabbits provided an important source of winter protein during this period, and the warrens were often a feature of a medieval landowner's possessions.

'Behind the headland to our left, are the remains of Dunraven Castle, which was finally destroyed in 1968. In fact, there have been four castles here. They were made of wood, however, until the Eleventh Century stone one was built. The castle is partly overgrown now by ivy, with handsome nodding thistles on the more open areas. Interestingly, there are some clumps of Hound's Tongue, a sand dune plant with attractive wine-red flowers and very bristly fruits which have a habit of sticking onto people's clothes. This means that they can turn up anywhere, and it is possible that the people who used to live here brought them home by accident from nearby sand dunes. The leaves of the plant are the shape of a hound's tongue, and it was believed that if you put a leaf in your sock or between your sock and your shoe you would be protected from being bitten by hounds – but I don't think I'd rely on it too much!'

As we climbed to the crest of the headland past a gnarled hawthorn, whose outline seemed to be following the contours of the land, Mary described the geology which had shaped the cliffs.

'The main type of rocks here are two different forms of limestone. The 350 million year old Carboniferous Limestone is

much the harder, and forms the base of the headland that we are on. The Blue Liassic Limestone, by comparison, is a mere 190 million years old, and erodes more easily. Two further kinds of liassic limestone were formed here on the shore of the ancient sea. The Blue Liassic rock has a smooth texture and does not have pebbles incorporated in it as it was laid down further out in deeper water. The two limestones would not be expected to occur together, as there is an enormous time span separating them. How-

These mounds on the cliff top are the remains of an Iron Age promontory fort. They would have been circular originally but as much as half of the fort has disappeared into the sea as the cliffs have eroded away.

A superb view of the wave-cut platform stretching along the coast. It is the old base of the cliffs which has escaped the full brunt of erosion by the sea.

ever, all the layers laid down in between, including the Coal Measures, have long since worn away again, and we are here left with what is known as an unconformity.

'Towards the east, there is a really breathtaking view along the cliffs, showing magnificent bedding and erosion which geologists come a long way to see. A particularly exciting feature, visible at low tide, is the great wave-cut rock platform stretching out to sea from the base of the cliffs. This can be looked at as a map of the horizontal strata uncluttered by vegetation – something we seldom see. It is the old base of the cliffs,

and it goes out nearly a quarter of a mile. Wave erosion occurs around the level of high tides, so rock below this level remains intact, while that above cracks, collapses and is washed away, causing the cliff to recede. The beds are slightly tilted so that you can walk along the platform, apparently going upstairs all the time, but actually staying on the same level. If you look back at the cliffs, you can see that they are horizontally banded, consisting of broad layers of creamy sandstone and narrower ones of black shale. No-one knows quite how this happens. Most geologists favour the idea of

a resorting of the rock after deposition as being more feasible than a regular pendulum swing of two different types of rock being deposited in sequence over millions of years. When the waves crash against these cliffs they cut back first along the narrower shale layers, leaving the more massive beds unsupported. The rocks are cleft by vertical joints, so it only takes a little of this undermining before a whole section comes tumbling down. If you look along the base of the cliffs, you can see great piles of rubble where this has happened recently, so take care. Don't get too close, either on top or

underneath! Big piles of rubble protect the base of the cliff from further erosion for a spell, but eventually they are washed away and transformed into further ammunition for the waves to hurl at the cliff and do more damage.

'The edges of these cliffs are remarkably square. Usually when one looks at a cliff edge it is rounded off by weathering. But with limestones, dissected by vertical joints, the rain seeps down into underground rivers or runs along the surface of an impermeable bed which is known as an aquifer. The wet patches on the cliffs are where

Top **Waves pounding up against the cliffs at high tide. The tremendous force of these waves has shaped these cliffs over the centuries.**

Above **Looking up at the cliffs from the wave-cut platform. The horizontal bedding is very marked. The bright green patch shows where an underground aquifer is seeping out.**

the water is seeping out from these aquifers. Because the rain is penetrating into the cliffs rather than rolling over the edge, there is no rounding off at the brink.

'The water, when it does come out, deposits a substance known as tufa, which is lime thrown out of solution, and is the same material that forms calcite "curtains" on the walls of caves and stalactites and stalagmites. When the water emerges into the air the calcium bicarbonate which it has dissolved while underground gives off carbon dioxide to leave insoluble calcium carbonate or limestone. Where this is happening, the cliff face is building up on a small scale, instead of being eroded away and there are some fascinating plants associated with this, which we will look at later on.

'Other interesting features along here are two hanging valleys. These are river valleys where the amount of water flowing on the surface is so small that it is unable to cut the valley down to sea level as quickly as the sea is cutting back inland. So they look as if they have been chopped off a little way back up their river course, with the river toppling over the edge of the cliff as a waterfall.'

As we were standing taking in the magnificent view of the cliffs, we could see various birds hanging in the air, expertly playing the turbulent air currents to their advantage. Most of these were Herring Gulls, which Mary pointed out as nesting on some of the inaccessible cliff ledges. Before the area became so popular with walkers, there were Lesser Black-backed Gulls as well, nesting on the cliff tops. One of the more interesting birds soaring around the cliffs was the Fulmar – easily recognised by the way it glides with its wings held stiffly out at right angles. It is not a gull but a member of the petrel or 'tube-nose' family. If you get a clear view of it, you can see that, unlike the gulls, it has tubular nostrils along the top of its stout beak. The Fulmar does nest further west in Glamorgan on the Gower cliffs, and Mary told us that they had been sitting around on these cliffs prospecting for about five years now, so the chances are that they might start nesting soon. The species has been expanding its range in the British Isles gradually for many years and whereas at one time it only bred on the remote island of St Kilda it can now be found breeding around most of our coasts at suitable sites. More remote cliffs on off-shore islands and inaccessible headlands, provide ideal nesting for some of our more exciting seabirds –

Puffins, Razorbills, Guillemots, Kittiwakes and Cormorants, but in Glamorgan we have to go west, to Gower, for these. Others to be found on the Dunraven cliffs are two birds that have taken advantage of sites provided by man but which would originally have bred exclusively on sites like these. One of these is the House Martin, which has several colonies on these cliffs where it plasters its nest to the cliff face in much the same way that it builds its nest under the eaves of houses. The other is the garrulous Jackdaw, a resident of chimney stacks in the mining valleys, which moves around noisily here in small flocks, nesting in crevices of the cliff face.

A Kestrel hovered overhead, flying into the wind at the speed the wind was blowing it back, so that it seemed to remain motionless.

Having watched the birds for a while, we turned our attention to the short turf that is such a feature of cliff tops. We asked Mary to describe the plants.

'The short grass turf, which we crossed as we climbed up the hill, was not very remarkable, being quite heavily grazed and manured by sheep. As fertility increases with manuring so more and more of the limestone plants are pushed out in the course of competition for space, and more robust grasses come in. We noticed some calicoles or lime-lovers as we came up, such as Wild Carrot and Bird's Foot Trefoil, but there was far more of the hard inedible Crested Dog's Tail Grass. This is like wire, and the animals tend to leave it; as do all but the most efficient lawn mowers!

'On the crest of the hill here, though, the colour that one expects from these beautiful limestone plants does begin. I can see purple patches of Wild Thyme which flowers in June and July. There is Rock Rose spilling over the crags, which is obviously not worried terribly by the grazing pressure – although there are fewer sheep here in the summer because of the danger of them getting chased by holiday makers' dogs. Some of the grasses – the Golden Oat Grass, Quaking Grass and Crested Hair Grass – leave us in no doubt as to the high lime content of the very shallow soil covering the rocks. In fact, many of these plants are probably rooting down into the limestone itself. One of the immediate things that you notice is their tiny size. This dwarfing is due to a combination of soil drought, exposure and grazing. If you want to live successfully up here on these cliff tops, you have to stoop to conquer. For, if you think you are going to rise to greater heights, somebody will come along and chomp you off or trample on you or you will get killed back by a drought or a salt gale. In fact, if you really want to see these plants to their best effect, you should be on your knees or stomach. There are tiny pink-edged Daisies, delicate purple Dove's Foot Cranesbill, and lemon dandelion-like heads of Mouse-eared Hawkweed. Over here, we have the tiny Sea Hard Grass, which has very rigid spikes and with it is Lady's Bed-straw, a charming little plant with bright yellow flowers, which are at their best in mid-July.

'On some more broken parts of the face I can see a little plant with small white trumpet-like flowers. This is Eyebright, a member of the Foxglove family, although this may be difficult to believe when you see this inch-high midget. It is semi-parasitic, but has green chlorophyll for making its own carbohydrates. Its roots clamp onto the roots of grasses for further sustenance but people who have been investgating these plants have found Eyebright roots clamped onto other Eyebright roots, which is a bit like helping yourself up a hill by holding your own hand! Another plant here is Salad Burnet, which has balls of flowers, some with tassels of yellow stamens and some with shaggy red styles, sticking out to

catch the wind-borne pollen. This, too, is a plant generally found only on grassy places with a lime-rich soil.

'This short turf is ideal for Rabbits, as long grasses tend to become damp – something they can't tolerate. Their burrows tunnel into the friable soil between the shattered limestone strata. Plants like the Small-flowered Buttercup, Parsley Piert and Scarlet Pimpernel thrive on the bare soil around the burrows. They need the exposed soil to root down, as they are

A Herring Gull (*Larus argentatus*) **hanging in the air near the cliff top. These gulls are great opportunists and have expanded their population recently taking full advantage of the excesses of man, as the large flocks at rubbish tips and quaysides testify.**

Jackdaw (*Corvus monedula***) on a cliff top. These members of the crow family are equally at home soaring around cliff ledges or church steeples. Like the House Martins, which have adapted to nesting under the eaves of our houses, their natural home is probably inaccessible cliff faces.**

A collection of colourful plants from the headland turf.
Above **Lady's Bedstraw** (*Galium verum*) **with Mouse-ear Hawkweed** (*Hieracium pilosella*).
Above right **Eyebright,** a group of plants which need the expert touch to identify correctly.
However, all experts have to make a start: so here's *Euphrasia officinalis.* Middle **Wild Thyme** (*Thymus drucei*), showing its beautiful purple flowers.
Right **Rock Rose** (*Helianthemum nummularium*), a plant of chalk grasslands and scrub.

annuals and are unable to get a roothold among the tightly bunched grasses of the turf. So there are some plants that benefit from the activities of Rabbits, even though they may be in danger of being eaten or scratched up!'

We then made our way round towards the tip of the headland. As we walked along, Mary pointed out more of the plants and insects that were enjoying the sunny aspect of the slope.

'There is a nice mixture of taller limestone plants here – yellow spikes of Agrimony, pink heads of Marjoram, and Corn Mint which will be flowering later on. Now, Marjoram and Mint are both members of the Labiate family, the "dead-nettles", which are rich in aromatic oils. We enjoy the scent, as do the butterflies and bees, which come for the nectar, but Rabbits don't like it, and leave them well alone. There are some splendid plants of pink Common Centaury and the rarer Yellow-wort; both of which belong to the Gentian family. The Yellow-wort is seldom found away from limey soil. One of the remarkable things about this species is the way the leaves grow in pairs but are joined together so that the stem seems to come up through the middle of a single saucer-like leaf. But if you look carefully, you will find that two little buds are coming out opposite each other, obviously one in the axil of each leaf. Teasel and Red Valerian are other plants which have leaves like this.

'South-facing slopes in this often balmy climate and with such a wealth of wild flowers are, of course, marvellous places for insects. On the right day, the whole place is buzzing with life. Butterflies, particularly if the wind is not too bad, are found all over the slope. One of the most frequent here is the Common Blue which likes to feed on the Bird's Foot Trefoil and clovers, Small Heaths also like these open places, as do Large and Small Skippers. Interestingly, when the Skippers settle, they hold their fore-wings up at an angle above the hind wings instead of putting the two together. The male Large Skipper is easy to identify as he has an oblique brown line across each orange fore-wing. This is made up of scent scales which attract the female to him. The Grayling is a larger butterfly often found along the cliffs. Occasionally, these butter-flies carry little red mites, but you need to have sharp eyes to spot them.

'If you sit here and watch, you will cer-

Top **The headland turf starred with tiny flowers and grasses. Their small size is due to a combination of salt-laden winds, soil drought and grazing pressure.**

Left **Amongst the larger grasses further down the slope are some members of the gentian family like this clump of Common Centaury** (*Centaurium erythraea*).

tainly see black and yellow hoverflies and droneflies feeding on the flowers. They are "dressed up" to look like wasps, but are quite harmless and have evolved in this way to fool would-be predators. They are real masters of flight; able to hover absolutely stationary or to dart backwards, and are almost impossible to follow with the eye when they decide to move to a new hovering position.

'From our great height of five or six feet, we tend to tramp through the countryside and miss an awful lot. So it is really worth sometimes getting down to the level of this other world. Here, for instance, in the shelter of the herbage, are several kinds of snails. A habitat like this, with so much lime being cycled out of the soil and into the plants, is ideal for snails as they need the extra ration of lime to build their shells. One rather interesting one you find here is the Land Winkle, which can close its shell with

an operculum or lid, like the periwinkles down on the seashore.'

We made our way across the ridge to the edge of the north facing cliff. From here a particularly verdant spot with water seeping out of the cliff to form a tufa flow was visible on the mainland cliff at the base of the headland. Some of it was covered with cushions of bright green mosses, starred with various flowers. So, having looked at flowers on our hands and knees, we now switched to looking at those on this inaccessible face through binoculars! Mary described the scene.

'Quite a few flowers grow on this tufa, but the main clumps are watercress, white with blossoms. The other white flowers belong to Brookweed. This is a freshwater plant, but it nearly always grows beside the sea as it likes a certain amount of salt spray in the air. There is also Common Scurvy Grass, its white flowers do not have the purplish tinge seen in the Danish Scurvy Grass of the clifftop turf. On the drier areas are Sea Mayweed and Wild Privet, with Hemp Agrimony on the damp areas between.

'Rock Pipits come here frequently to feed because, of course, all the water and vegetation nurtures a rich invertebrate life. They catch insect larvae which they feed to their chicks in a crevice nest higher up the cliff.'

From this point, we walked down the springy turf towards the low point of the headland, noting the changes as we approached the tip.

'There is a subtle change in the turf here which shows up nicely in the summer when everything is flowering. Most of the turf sweeping down from the top of the ridge is made up of bent and fescue grasses, Crested Dog's Tail and a lot of White Clover with Thyme, Rock Rose, Ribwort Plantain, and so on. But as you get down to the tip of the headland, the pink heads of Thrift come marching up from the seaward fringe. Also, Buck's Horn Plantain, with its rosettes of lobed leaves, takes over from the Ribwort Plantain; Sea Storksbill replaces the Dove's Foot Cranesbill and the Red Fescue becomes short and crimped, with curly leaves. Some of it is quite greyish – a special glaucous seaside form which you get in exposed habitats. Sea Pearlwort replaces the Ciliate Pearlwort, and eventually where the turf gives way to rock we start to come across Rock Sea Lavender and the Rock Samphire growing in crevices with Yellow Stonecrop. While the Thrift is an early spring flower,

Brookweed (*Samolus valerandi*) **amongst the rocks. This plant is a freshwater species but nearly always grows beside the sea as it likes a certain amount of salt spray. This specimen is interesting as it has developed a strap-like stem. This is called fasciation, and can be caused as a result of a gall-like infestation or a genetical abnormality of the plant itself.**

the Sea Lavender, which is a near relative, flowers much later in the year and is only just starting to bloom in June. The Rock Samphire has fleshy cream-coloured flowers and quite succulent red fruits which persist into November and December.

'Below this, there is nothing between us and the sea, except two bands of lichens: uppermost is the orange lichen zone, below it, before we enter the marine environment, is the black lichen zone, which is sometimes mistaken for oil stains – a sign of the times.'

As we walked along the rock platform on top of this low cliff, Mary pointed out several interesting features on the rock surface.

'If you look at the rock, you'll see black "pebbles" buried in it. This is chert, which is to limestone what flint is to chalk; in other words, siliceous inclusions in a calcareous matrix. Some of the other marks are fossil brachiopods, which are rather like our modern bivalves. Some of them are corals. When this rock was formed, it was 15° South of the Equator and the climate was typically tropical. This is why quite a lot of these fossils are corals, and all the fossilized life-forms here certainly came from coral seas. On liassic rock on the beach, you might find the whirligig-shaped ammonite fossils for which this coast, like the liassic cliffs of Dorset, is famous. The white streaks are usually infillings of calcite. They are sometimes called tension gashes, and indicate where the rock has been very contorted and the calcite has subsequently seeped into the cracks.'

Walking back around to the more sheltered south-east side of the headland, we could see the vegetation on the lower slopes was much ranker than the short sward on top. Mary pointed out that, because of the long history of grazing along that part of the land, the main plants were, by and large, the ones that had proved unpalatable to the sheep. These were thistles, including the rare Woolly Thistle, with its magnificent heads and prickly three-dimensional leaves. There were also stands of that notoriously poisonous plant, Hemlock. This is the plant

Above left **Rock Sea Lavender** (*Limonium binervosum*) **growing out from a rock crevice. This near-relative of Thrift provides a welcome splash of colour on our rock ledges in mid-summer. It grows as far north as Wigtown and follows you south to your holiday in Spain and Portugal.**

Above right **Buck's Horn Plantain** (*Plantago cororopus*). **This is a typical plant of our coasts and gets its name from the distinctive leaves. The rosette growth form, protects it from both grazing pressure and desiccation by the wind**

Musk Thistle (*Carduus nutans*) **silhouetted against the sky. Their sharp spines have protected them against grazing by sheep.**

A bristletail (*Petrobius maritimus*) on the cliff face. These primitive insects scavenge along the splash zone, indicated here by the bright orange lichen, *Caloplaca*.

A calcite curtain deposited by water seeping out from an underground aquifer. These curtains are formed in the same way as the stalagtites of underground cave systems.

that put an end to Socrates' philosophising. It is a member of the Umbelliferae and has the characteristic 'umbrella' of white flowers, but you can recognise it by the purple spots on the stem. Lower down, there were drifts of Stinking Iris. Mary described them.

'There are a lot of these irises about in mid-summer. The flowers are as large as a garden iris, but their colour is a rather anaemic purple. Later on, the capsules open to expose lovely orange seeds which persist all winter. The name Stinking Iris is unfair, to my mind, as they don't stink at all. If you break a leaf and rub it between your fingers you will get an appetising smell of cold roast beef and it is sometimes called the "Roast Beef Plant".

'A much more special plant is the Stinking Hellebore. This is really poisonous but again, I don't think it stinks. It has very handsome flowers early in February, greenish-yellow with purple edges, turning to clusters of upright capsules by April. Another plant which is unpalatable here, is the Spurge Laurel, which isn't a laurel or a

spurge, but is a member of the Daphne family. This again flowers early in February, with little green flowers and has shiny evergreen leaves. This is really a woodland plant, and it is quite tolerant of the shade under the dense shrubs at the bottom of the slope, but will suffer from "wind-scorch" in the open.'

We made our way along the coast path that cut between some thick shrubby plants. The most notable was Sea Buckthorn, which is a native of the East Coast and usually found on sand dunes, where it is notoriously aggressive. These shrubs have been planted on the old castle estate. Further on, we came upon some other 'aliens' – Holm Oak, Bay Trees and Tamarisk. This last tree is frequently planted along seaside promenades because of its salt tolerance. Mary described it as a rather feathery-leaved plant, with tassels of pink flowers. The floor by the path was covered in places with Periwinkles, another relict of the old estate.

A vole feeding on Sea Hard Grass (*Parapholis strigosa*) **amongst the rocks. The waves were making such a noise that the photographer was able to sit and watch this little mammal eating its lunch without it knowing.**

Woolly Thistle (*Cirsium eriphorum* **subspecies** *brittanicum*)**, a nice plant to find wherever it grows, for it always indicates lime-rich conditions and hence, a great variety of other plants.**

Wild Cabbage
(*Brassica oleracea*), the
ancestor of our garden
varieties, growing in
its native habitat – an
inaccessible slope
away from the hungry
rabbits and sheep.

As we came out onto a more open stretch of the cliff walk, we could see some interesting cabbagy looking plants. Mary explained.

'Three of our commonest vegetables come from sea cliff plants – Wild Cabbage, Wild Carrot and Sea Beet. All of them are growing here and the Wild Cabbages are particularly healthy looking. These are characteristic along the ledges of the liassic cliffs; both here and in South Dorset. The Wild Cabbage, as its name implies, has delectably succulent cabbage-like leaves, and, because of the profusion of Rabbits along the cliff top, it has become a cliff-face plant, growing where the Rabbits cannot reach it.'

Before heading back, we climbed down the cliff and crossed the bay, with its wave cut platform, to have a closer look at one of the tufa flows. When we arrive, Mary pointed out a rather special plant.

'Growing in the crevices up amongst the tufa is a very novel plant – the Maidenhair Fern. Although rare in Britain, this is scattered all along the Heritage Coast cliffs, but is found only where the water seeps out from the rocks into these tufa flows. It is usually a plant of the tropics or sub-tropics, and it has always been a puzzle as to how it can survive in a place like this, where we have frosts. The answer was brought home to me while walking along these cliffs in January 1980. All the aquifers had curtains of icicles, except where the Maidenhair Fern was growing. Suddenly the penny dropped – the water coming from underground was coming out at a constant temperature, probably about 50°F, whether it was summer or winter, and this constancy was enabling the fern to survive.'

The tufa flow itself is very gelatinous at the surface and is coloured green in places. This is significant because, although the deposition of the lime salts can be entirely chemical, it is very often a biological process as well, helped by the green plants which grow in the water. Blue-green algae are particularly important, but higher up the cliff mosses are also at work. They are actively extracting carbon dioxide from the water for photosynthesis, and in doing so are releasing more of the calcium carbonate from the calcium bicarbonate in solution. So quite often the deposits on the cliff face are due, in part, to plants, and their pale green colour to the incorporation of accumulations of microscopic algae.

'Some of the more salt tolerant cliff plants like Red Fescue get right down onto shelves below the tufa, where they must be completely drowned by seawater at high tide.

Maidenhair Fern (*Adiantum capillus-veneris*), one of those botanical treasures that everyone hopes to find one day growing in the wild. It is highly specific to sheltered cliff sites and tufa flows in western Britain.

This glistening tufa flow has microscopic algae incorporated in it. These extract carbon dioxide from the water for their photosynthesis and give the rock surface a slippery gelatinous texture.

Yet evidently the freshwater dripping out of the rocks is sufficient to neutralise any bad effect of the salt and keep them going.'

Having climbed back up to the clifftop we wandered gently back in the valley behind the headland to the sandy beach where we began. Along the way we stopped off to explore a marvellous old walled-garden with Ivy-leaved Toadflax and Wall Pennywort growing over the walls. We had seen a tremendous number of plants exploiting the potential of the limestone cliffs, on our walk. The stooping trees and the tiny size of many of the plants testified to the dominant forces of the wind and salt-laden air, but the main impression that we kept with us as we set off for home was of those splendid carpets of wild flowers of all colours – and the next time I go for a cliff walk, I know that I shall be looking out for these again.

Rocky Shorelines

To me and many thousands of marine biologists John Barrett is a very special person. He and his team at Dale Fort in Pembrokeshire have introduced many of us to the wonders of marine life. Here he is in splendid form walking with care and immense knowledge across his home patch, the wonderfully rich rocky shore at Dale. The only thing that is missing from the real experience is the cry of the gulls and the taste of good Welsh tea at the end of a satisfying day in the field.

The rocky shoreline at Dale, covered in seaweeds and providing a home for a vast array of animals.

Information

Zonation

The regular ebb and flow of the tides along our coasts is one of the dominant forces determining the distribution of its plant and animal life (see page 14). Rocky shores with their relatively fixed surfaces and sheltered crevices and rock pools can be exceptionally rich in marine life and are very rewarding places to explore. One of the main characteristics of these shores is the vertical zonation of the animals and plants. Those in the splash zone, for example, at the top of the shore are adapted to spending most of their lives out of water, whereas those on the lower shore are adapted to living predominantly below water. A few animals are able to exploit a wide spectrum of these zones but the majority have clearly defined distributions which are indicated in the diagram. An important point to bear in mind when studying this zonation is that the profile and exposure of the shore can alter it considerably. A near vertical slope will have a very truncated zonation (see page 20), whilst a flat shore such as a wave-cut platform will have a greatly extended one. Rock pools can also distort the overall pattern as their permanent water can provide homes for lower shore animals on the upper shore. However, those pools on the upper shore are subjected to great extremes and may support no more than some strands of the ubiquitous *Enteromorpha*. Remember, if you turn over any rocks while looking for animals be sure to replace them carefully. The animals have deliberately chosen the protection of the rock and could die if left exposed for too long, and be careful not to squash them as you put the rock back.

Sites

Rocky shores are a feature of coasts dominated by erosion and are more typically found along our 'high' coasts in western and northern Britain. The following is a selection of some interesting sites and is obviously not meant as a general guide as excellent stretches of rocky shore can be found almost anywhere along our coasts.

St Abbs Head, Borders. The wave-cut platform beneath the towering Old Red Sandstone cliffs support a rich littoral and sub-littoral fauna. Scottish Wildlife Trust Reserve.
Purbeck Peninsula, Dorset. Interesting variety of seashore life. Marine reserve at Kimmeridge Bay.
Start Point, Devon. Good area for rocky shores as well as sandy bays; excellent area for seaweeds.
Cornwall Coast Path. Exciting areas of rocky shoreline can be found all around the Cornish coast. Anyone planning to explore the area should consult the *Cornish Coast Path* by E. C. Pyatt. HMSO.
Welcombe and Marshland Reserve, Devon. This stretch of the coast was described by E. Arber in 1911 when he wrote: 'It may be doubted whether any other shore line in Britain furnishes as many and as perfect examples of folded and contorted rocks as these.'
Gower Peninsula, Glamorgan. The south side of this highly interesting peninsula provides many good stretches of rocky shoreline.
Pembroke Coast Path, Dyfed. This area has some of the most interesting stretches of rocky shoreline in western Britain. Anyone wishing to explore this coast should consult *The Pembroke Coast Path* by John Barrett. HMSO.
Menai Straits, Gwynedd. The combined effects of the sheltered position and strong tides make this strait extremely rich in littoral species.
South Ardnamurchan coast, Argyll. An area of rocky shores and also the most westerly point of the Scottish mainland.
Loch Scavaig, Skye. An example of the many interesting inlets and lochs along the western Scottish coast which have a rich and varied coastal fauna and flora.

	Seaweeds	Molluscs	Crustaceans	Others
Splash Zone			Ligia oceanica	Lichen zone
Upper Shore	Pelvetia canaliculata	Littorina neritoides	Orchestia gammarella	
Mid-shore	Fucus spiralis Ascophyllum nodosum Fucus vesiculosus	Littorina saxatilis Monodonta lineata Littorina littorea Nucella lapillus Littorina littoralis Mytilus edulis Gibbula umbilicalis	Carcinus maenas Balanus balanoides	Actinia equina Spirorbis borealis
Lower Shore	Fucus serratus	Gibbula cineraria		Halichondria panicea Pomatoceros triqueter Membranipora membranacea
Sub-littoral Zone	Laminaria spp.			Echinus esculentus

Some plants and animals of our rocky shores

Plants

Sea Lettuce *Ulva lactuca*
Intestine Weed *Enteromorpha intestinalis*
Channelled Wrack *Pelvetia canaliculata*
Spiral Wrack *Fucus spiralis*
Bladder Wrack *Fucus vesiculosus*
Serrated Wrack *Fucus serratus*
Smooth-stalked Kelp *Laminaria digitata*
Rough-stalked Kelp *Laminaria hyperborea*
Crinkled Kelp *Laminaria saccharina*
Purple Laver *Porphyra umbilicalis*

Fishes

Some small fishes can often be found in the deeper rock pools on the lower shore. These include blennies (*Blennius*) and gobies (*Gobius*).

Birds

Cormorant *Phalacrocorax carbo*
Oystercatcher *Haematopus ostralegus*
Turnstone *Arenaria interpres*
Purple Sandpiper *Calidris maritima*
Herring Gull *Larus argentatus*
Rock Pipit *Anthus spinoletta*

Invertebrates

Breadcrumb Sponge *Halichondria panicea*
Sea Fir *Gonothyraea loveni*
Beadlet Anemone *Actinia equina*
Snakelocks Anemone *Anemonia sulcata*
Green Paddleworm *Eulalia viridis*
Spirorbis borealis
Pomatoceros triqueter
Limpet *Patella vulgata*
Topshells *Gibbula, Monodonta*
Winkles *Littorina*
Dogwelk *Nucella lapillus*
Mussel *Mytilus edulis*
Acorn Barnacle *Balanus balanoides*
Sandhopper *Orchestia gammarella*
Sea Slater *Ligia oceanica*
Broad-clawed Porcelain Crab *Porcellana platycheles*
Shore Crab *Carcinus maenas*
Springtail *Lipura maritima*
Sea Mat *Membranipora membranacea*
Star Ascidian *Botryllus schlosseri*

Sea Slaters (*Ligia oceanica*) **on the rocky shoreline.**

Rocky Shorelines

with John Barrett

One of the most exciting places for a naturalist to explore is a stretch of rocky coastline at low tide. Britain has some superb lengths, particularly along our northern and western coasts. We went down to one of the many lovely bays on the Pembrokeshire coast to see what we could find. Our guide for the day was John Barrett, who has written and lectured on the life of our shores for many years and who was co-author of the first field guide to the animals and plants living there.

We started our walk as the tide was going out across a slippery belt of seaweeds. Before we went too far, we asked John to describe some of the problems of living in this habitat and something of the principles that controlled the distribution of plants and animals in it.

'Probably only the coral reefs of the world contain as great a variety of types of plants and animals as live on a rocky shore. This variety includes representatives of all the major groups in the animal kingdom (the Phyla). Since all are animals of the sea and not of the land, they all breathe oxygen which is dissolved in seawater. Also many feed directly on that primary source of food in the sea – the plankton.

'Drifting in the surface layers of the sea are living organisms in numbers beyond computation. At least 800 animals, each larger than a bacterium, will be in the next mouthful of seawater the reader swallows when swimming. These are the 'flesh' – the meat – of the plankton.

'When the prophet cried that all flesh was grass he was searching for consolation and not asserting a biological truth. Nonetheless all flesh in the sea depends for food on microscopically small single-celled plants called diatoms – 20 000 of the largest and several millions of the smaller in a bucketful. Diatoms aggregate a greater weight per acre of sea than do fully grown potatoes in an acre of field. They far outnumber the animals in that mouthful of seawater. Diatoms are the first link of every food chain in the sea and on the shore.

'The dangers of living on a rocky shore are considerable. First of all, being marine, the animals must never dry out. So all are adapted in one way or another to resist desiccation by wind and/or sun when the ebb tide has left them in the open air. They also have to avoid being washed away during a gale. The gale may rage for two days, with twenty tons of water in each cubic yard of each wave crashing onto the shore. Then, next day, when all is quiet again, the little animals are exactly where they were before the gale blew up.

'The ebb and flow of the tide is a dominant control in the distribution of life along a rocky shore. Tidal characteristics confine many common plants and animals within horizontal layers – the technical word is 'zonation'. Nothing shows zonation on a shore better than the big brown seaweeds called the wracks.

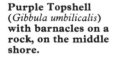

Purple Topshell (*Gibbula umbilicalis*) **with barnacles on a rock, on the middle shore.**

'At the top, around mean high water of spring tides, is a zone dominated by the Channelled Wrack, *Pelvetia canaliculata*; just below, at mean high water neaps, is the Flat Wrack, *Fucus spiralis*. In the middle of the shore is a layer of Egg Wrack, *Ascophyllum nodosum*, which, where it is sheltered from waves, lies over the rocks as a dense mattress, almost excluding all other plants and animals. Below the Egg Wrack comes the Bladder Wrack, *Fucus vesiculosus*, with its paired bladders which pop so readily when dry. Then lower down again, at about low water of neaps, is the Saw Wrack, *Fucus serratus*, which is easily identified by the edge of the frond having teeth along it rather like those of a saw.

'This outline pattern of zonation is complicated by wave action. For instance, Egg Wrack is mechanically feeble. A mass of it may dominate the middle of a sheltered shore, but, as soon as the angle changes to admit a greater pressure of wave action, the Egg Wrack is increasingly torn away by those waves. Even small waves shorten it to the point that it cannot brush off the barnacle larvae from the rocks at that delicate moment when they settle as adults from the plankton. As the exposure increases the length of the wracks decreases, so the area of open rock surface increases, allowing the number of barnacles to increase until they dominate the exposed shore from about the middle downwards. A square yard of surface may accommodate up to 60000 barnacles. The number along a mile of coast is, indeed, large.

'The zonation of winkles is easy to see. In the splash zone, above high water mark, is the tiny Small Winkle, *Littorina neritoides*. Lower down, at much the same level as the Flat Wrack, comes the Rough Winkle, *Littorina saxatilis*. (Some specialists argue nowadays that this one name may cover four separate species.) At midtide level on less exposed shores is the Edible Winkle, *Littorina littorea*; slightly lower, with the Bladder Wrack, comes the Flat Winkle, *Littorina littoralis*, which is coloured either dark black-green or bright yellow.

'These Flat Winkles are much the same size and shape as the bladders in Bladder Wrack. Until quite recently it was thought that, at low tide, the 'yellow' winkles hid from hungry waders underneath the seaweeds while the 'green' ones stayed on top, made safe from detection by their shape and colour. By the simple test of counting the

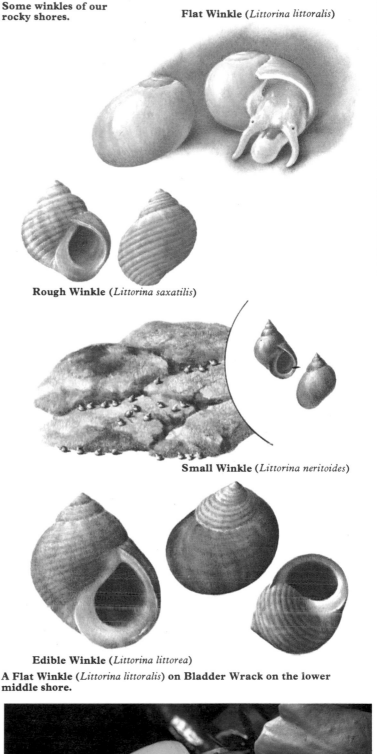

Some winkles of our rocky shores.

Flat Winkle (*Littorina littoralis*)

Rough Winkle (*Littorina saxatilis*)

Small Winkle (*Littorina neritoides*)

Edible Winkle (*Littorina littorea*)

A Flat Winkle (*Littorina littoralis*) **on Bladder Wrack on the lower middle shore.**

numbers of the two colours on and under a sample patch of wracks anybody can confirm that this hard worn notion is not true!

'Like all the other winkles, the Small are male or female. They copulate and then release fertilized eggs. Living so high up the shore, there is a biological advantage if all the Small Winkles in one area synchronize this release to coincide with the time of high-water spring-tides in winter, just at the time when there is the greatest chance that splash from a gale will wash down those eggs into the sea. There they hatch, and then pass through their various larval stages in the plankton which precede settlement as adults on the shore. At the time of settlement they have a magic capability (instinct) within them. When covered by water they crawl upwards; when becoming uncovered by the ebb tide they move into dark cracks in the rocks. This gives protection from passing predators. Then, when the new flood covers them again, the urge to climb reasserts dominance over the urge to hide in the dark; so up they go again. In the end they find their way right up to the top of the shore. A remarkable journey for a snail which may be less than a fifth of an inch long (5 millimetres).

'The Rough Winkle avoids these hazards by giving birth to fully developed young. Although living at a slightly lower level on the shore than the Small, the Rough has a second advantage in the evolutionary race out of the sea onto the land. Its gills show the first signs of modification towards being lungs. It can 'breathe' very damp air. So, in, say, a million more years, we may find Rough Winkles amongst our lettuces!

'The Rough is well adapted to resist all degrees of wave action. A snail's shell is made up of a series of whorls. Given a snail's shape and asked how it could be strengthened to resist the hammer blows from stones crashed onto it during a gale, a mechanical engineer would say that the incision between successive whorls must be deepened. This is just how evolution (survival of the fittest) has worked in the Rough Winkle. Compare one from a very exposed shore with one from shelter and it is hard to believe that the two specimens belong to the same species. However, a series of shells collected in a sequence from exposure to shelter will show a gradation of modification (adaptation) linking the two ends of the series (a biological cline).

'The topshells, common on all but very exposed rocky shores, are different from the winkles in that they do not copulate, but release their sperm and ova into the sea. Fertilization then depends upon the chance meeting in the sea of the ovum with a sperm, which are meanwhile at risk in the food chains.

'Another difference between winkles and topshells is that topshells have a little hole in the centre of the mouth of the shell which indicates the hollowness of the column round which the shell is built. Since winkles have a column which is solid, they have no hole in the middle of their mouths.

'The topshells do not come as high up the beach as the winkles. On many, the Purple, *Gibbula umbilicalis*, flourishes at about mean sea level and the Grey, *G. cineraria*, downwards from low water of neaps. The

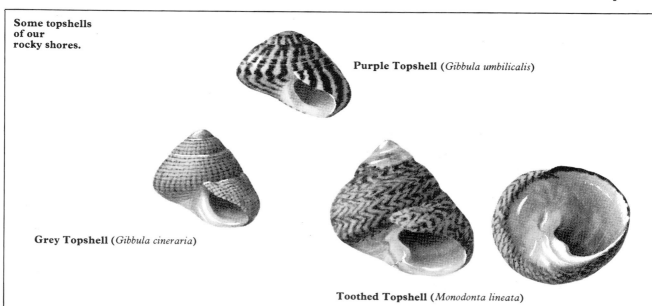

Some topshells of our rocky shores.

Purple Topshell (*Gibbula umbilicalis*)

Grey Topshell (*Gibbula cineraria*)

Toothed Topshell (*Monodonta lineata*)

Toothed Topshell, *Monodonta lineata*, has a shining mother-of-pearl mouth and zig-zag markings on its shell. It is otherwise much the same size and colour as the Edible Winkle, which is found in the same places.

'A feature common to both winkles and topshells (and many other snails and worms) is the operculum. When the animal pulls itself into its shell, the entrance is stoppered by a round leathery disc. This operculum holds in moisture, so saving the owner from being dried out. It is also an effective barrier against entry by a hungry predator.

'The limpet is an animal characteristic of all rocky shores. The conical shell can be as much as 2 inches (6 centimetres) across but it is usually somewhat smaller than that. The limpet clings to the rock by a sucker foot with proverbial tightness. Each lives in its own 'home' which is ground out by circular muscular pressure to fit the shell precisely to the rock. Soft rock is ground to fit the shell; but the shell is ground to fit hard rock. So, no matter what the nature of the rock, there is always a watertight fit between it and the limpet shell. Just before the ebb tide exposes the animal to the danger of desiccation the shell is pulled down tight onto its home, so retaining water in the tissues of the limpet and in the empty spaces in the shell round the body. Even so, all the oxygen in the trapped water would be used up before the returning tide could replace it, if it were not for the limpet's ability to lift its shell that fractional distance from the rock that allows oxygen from the air to percolate in but does not allow the water inside to leak out.

'When the tide covers them, limpets move about feeding. They have, like the winkles and topshells, a long tongue on which are hard chitinous teeth. It is a nice coincidence of organic chemistry that these teeth are of the same material as the hard wing-cases of beetles. The limpet tongue is rolled out and then withdrawn so that the hooked teeth on the underside scrape off diatoms lodged on the rock or slivers from the surface of larger seaweeds which are then ingested by the limpets.

'When on these feeding sorties they travel several feet from their "home", but they

The tell-tale signs of a limpet grazing. They feed on the minute single-celled algae which coat the surface of the rock.

Limpets (*Patella*). The one on its back shows its sucker-foot, ringed by its gills, with its head and tentacles protruding to the left. Dogwhelks have eaten some of the barnacles. The grey patch is the calcium carbonate base from which all the plant cells of the seaweed, *Lithophyllum* sp., have died off, perhaps eaten by limpets.

Rocky shore dominated by Acorn Barnacles (*Balanus bàlanoides***) and so exposed that only residual tufts of wracks just survive.**

always return to it before the ebb tide exposes them again. It is easy to test the ability of limpets to return to their homes from various distances and angles. Gently knock off two or three and mark them with spots of nail varnish. Dab the same code of spots beside their "home", from which you tapped them. Now put the limpets a measured distance away in some damp place – sideways, upwards or downwards. When the tide comes in they will be off feeding; before it goes out again they will have secured themselves on their "homes" – up to a distance limit which your experiment will determine.

'We have already noted the wide zone of barnacles in the lower half of exposed shores. The barnacles' relationship to crabs and woodlice was not discovered until 1833 when their larval forms were first recognised. Up to then they were counted as molluscs. Most barnacle species have six external plates which are often fused together. An Australian invader with only four plates was first noticed in 1945. All species have two more plates within the protection of the outer ring which, when covered by the tide, slide open to allow "legs" to emerge which kick rhythmically to establish an in-flow of seawater laden with oxygen and food.

expose the surface of the rock to which it was attached. This exposure gives barnacle larvae the chance they need to attach themselves.

'Next Dogwhelks move in, which eat the barnacles. The mussel clumps developing round what was temporarily an area of living barnacles are now free to spread across the dead barnacles' shells, until, once more, the new mussel clump is washed off and the barnacles can again use the rock surface newly cleared of mussels. So the cycle turns.

'The attachment of mussels is by sticky threads which are extruded through the narrow end of the shell. The threads are something like the guy ropes of a tent but, unlike a tent's, they attach only the front end of the mussel. This leaves the shell free to flex to changing angles of the press of the waves. Had the shell been fixed firmly throughout its length, it would quickly have been smashed off by water pressure.

'Mussels feed by drawing in a flow of water through an inhalant tube ("siphon") extension of its body. Just as for so many

'On an exposed shore largely dominated by barnacles you often find a mass of mussels amongst them. The relationship between the density of mussels and the density of barnacles is intricate. The larval mussels, which are in the plankton, at the time of changing to adults are chemically attracted by the already existing attached adults and they fix themselves onto these adults. More and more come in, drawn to the same site by the 'scent', so that large lumps of mussels are built up, attached to the rock only by those at the bottom of the pile. Eventually the clump gets so big that a wave coming in at the critical angle can smash it off and so

other animals, barnacles, for instance, this water contains oxygen for breathing and plankton for food. Fine hair sieves attached to the mussel's gills separate the food from the fine silt and sand suspended in the water which falls down into the bottom of the shell until released into the sea by opening the shell.

'Meanwhile the food is carried from the filters into the digestive tract by the water flow. In its passage through the tissues of the mussel the water has had added to it eggs or sperm which are then squirted out through the exhalant siphon with the waste water. Each mussel passes a pint of seawater

Barnacles feeding. In effect, these crustaceans are attached to the rocks by their head ends and their thoracic appendages have become filter-feeding organs.

through itself every 12–15 minutes. The danger of sucking in water that was waste from a neighbour is avoided by all squirting out the waste with something like eight times the force available for sucking in. So waste is jetted too far out into the body of sea water to be recirculated until it has been recharged with food and oxygen.

'To ensure the stability of the adult population the chances that a mussel egg will be fertilized are increased by the release from the males of many times more sperms than the 25 million eggs emitted by each female. The chance is still further improved when all the adults synchronize this release with the time of the same summer spring tide.

'Despite the astronomical initial numbers twenty four hours later only 170,000 swimming larvae survive beneath each square yard of water over a mussel bed. Of these less than fifty survive to be adults. The rest have been eaten. For instance, each of those hundreds of thousands of acorn barnacles living hard by, constantly kick in a flow of water from which they extract as food, mussel eggs, sperm and larvae amongst all the other planktonic titbits. Those who

Mussels, barnacles, limpets and two much abraded Purple Top-shells, compete for space at about mean sea level on a rocky shore.

think that these reproductive processes are wasteful are thinking too narrowly of the species and not of the total community which are dependent on each other for food and thus for survival.

'The Dogwhelk, *Nucella lapillus*, is a common mollusc where barnacles flourish. It eats them. The Dogwhelk's thick, elongated and rough shell has a hollowed extension of the mouth through which a tube-tongue can be extruded, the end of which is rimmed with a circlet of hard points. The whelk forces its tongue against the thinner internal plates of the barnacle and screws an entrance by twisting its tongue. Then it can suck out the barnacle meat. Any population of barnacles contains many empty cases – all of them cleaned out by whelks.

'After copulation the female whelks deposit capsules of eggs in deep cracks at low tide level. They are massed together like stalked grains of wheat. Only five per cent of the 300–1 000 eggs in each are fertile. After some four months the remaining ninety-five per cent will have been eaten by the few that hatch and now emerge about 1/16th inch (1·5 millimetres) long. They do

not attack barnacles until they have grown to about a quarter of an inch (6 millimetres).

'Three or four little lumps are often to be seen in the mouth of a Dogwhelk shell. They indicate a period when the food supply was too scarce to allow steady growth. When food is plentiful the shell begins to expand again and those little lumps disappear up into the increasing size of the shell.'

Having looked at the commonest molluscs we moved down the shore to see what else was about. We quickly lit on some sea-anemones.

'The commonest anemone on rocky shores, and particularly in pools, is the dark crimson Beadlet, *Actinia equina*. The name comes from the circlet of cornflower-blue spots which you will see if you gently fold

Dogwhelk (*Nucella lapillus*) **feeding on Acorn Barnacles.**

Beadlet Anemone (*Actinia equina*); the protruding mouth can be seen at the centre of the tentacles.

Snakelocks Anemone (*Anemone sulcata*) above patches of the purple encrusting 'red' sea-weed, which lays down a base of molecules of calcium carbonate separated from sea-water, providing the security on which the plant cells of *Lithophyllum* develop.

brush against them. They then fold down upon the luckless meal and slowly force it towards and, then, into the mouth which is located within the circle of tentacles. Some anemones have spring-loaded narcotic darts attached within their body with which they can tranquillise a struggling captive and so prevent it damaging their mouth. The meal is then digested quietly and the waste material ejected.

'Some of the larger sea-slugs, including the Common Grey, *Aeolidia papillosa*, having eaten a sea-anemone, are able to separate out from the body of the anemone the stinging threads complete with the mechanism for their release and then to pass the whole apparatus up into their own back; what was the poisonous armament of the anemone now defends the slug that ate it.

'The Snakelocks, *Anemonia sulcata*, is common around mean sea level in rock pools. It is usually a rather dull khaki colour but some are magic apple green, with the tentacles shading through to an exquisite watery blue-purple tip. The Snakelocks cannot close up its tentacles; they constantly writhe in memory of Medusa.

'Although rock pools are such a feature of rocky shores it is misguided to expect that they always hold a lovely selection of plants and animals within them. The dangers of living in a pool are not at once obvious. For instance, summer sunshine may heat up the water far above the temperature of the sea; winter's cold may cool it equally far below

back the top of the column of the anemone. Out of water they are but blobs of dark red jelly, quite different from the flower-heads of tentacles that open when the tide returns.

'Anemones are simple animals, related to jellyfish. They have only one entrance to the body. This is the mouth at the time of feeding, but, when the meal has been digested, the inedible bits and the body waste are excreted through what was the mouth and is now the anus.

'Under water the sticky tentacles wave gently, waiting for some tiny animal to sea temperature; a pool may even freeze. Heavy rain may wash out all the salt water and leave the pool almost fresh; hot sunshine may evaporate the water to the point that it becomes supersaturated with salt, with salt crystals shining round the edge. Only a very few animals are adapted to survive such heavy physiological strains. Big, deep pools are the real treasure houses.

'However, on the surface of even quite small pools you may well find tiny blue creatures, either singly or, more often, aggregated in lumps supported by the surface tension of the water. These are wingless insects called *Lipura maritima*.

'All insects breathe atmospheric oxygen through little tubes in the side of their bodies. In *Lipura*, the cross-section of these tubes is so small that the surface tension prevents water from penetrating into them and so drowning the insect. To guard against being drowned, if it is washed back into the sea by waves and then held below the surface in a cold water layer, the insect's body is covered with downy hairs within which it traps bubbles of air that provide enough oxygen to last five days. So it has only to get its breath, so to speak, once in five days during which the chances are that it will have been washed back onto the shore again.'

We turned again to hunting among the rocks and seaweeds. John soon pulled out a fine Shore Crab, *Carcinus maenas*, its rich green shell glistening in the sunshine.

'You can readily recognise him because he is the only crab which has three blunt teeth between the eyes and five sharp ones on either side of the shell. The last joint of the back legs is flattened for swimming but is still sharply pointed enough for walking. In the true swimming crabs this last joint is as rounded as a paddle blade. The tail is tucked under the shell; the male's is narrow, pointed and 5-jointed; the female's roundly broad and 7-jointed. Under the female's tail you may find a sandy coloured, granular bunch of 150000 fertile eggs which she carries for several months before they hatch into planktonic larvae. After undergoing six changes of form in the sea they eventually settle as adult crabs about an eighth of an inch (3 millimetres) across.

'Carrying their "skeleton" outside their body they would be unable to grow larger were they not adapted to rid themselves periodically of its constriction. When the time comes to grow, the crab creeps for

Below **Springtails** (*Lipura maritima*) **are wingless insects, here supported by surface tension on the water of a pool; they are the only common intertidal insect.**

Bottom **Shore-crab** (*Carcinus maenas*) **amongst Sea-lettuce; the light is reflected off the three blunt teeth between the eyes and some of the sharp points on either side.**

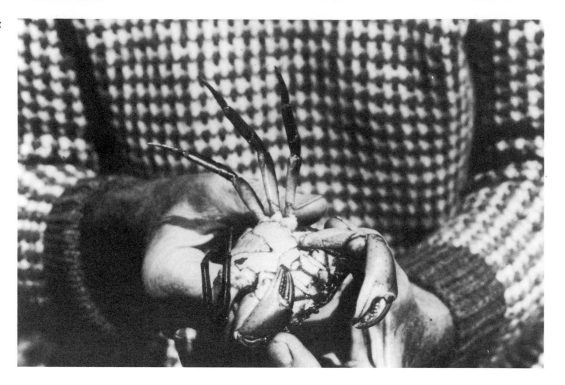

shelter under a rock or deep amongst sea-weeds and then the line of weakness, which runs along the back of the shell, is split open and the body forces out backwards. All is removed including the gills from the gill-covers, the eyes from their stalks and the legs are extricated right from the tip end. After three to four days the new shell will have hardened out, one third larger than the old one. Starting with a shell 3 millimetres across and increasing in size by a third at each change, how many changes does a crab undergo before it has reached its full size of 150 millimetres across?

'While most of the cast shells are quickly smashed to pieces by the waves, some, caught by currents, accumulate along the high tide line of saltmarshes and in very sheltered nooks along a rocky shore. If you find such an accumulation you will know that no catastrophe has smitten the local crabs, when you note that all the shells are split along the line at the back.

'Sometimes you will find under the tail of a crab, not a granular lump of eggs, but a smooth, grey mass which is the reproductive parts of a parasitic barnacle, *Sacculina carcini*. This parasite has larval stages exactly like the acorn barnacles', but, at the change to the adult state, instead of settling on rocks it settles on a crab's jaws from where it grows threads throughout the host's tissues through which the parasite absorbs food. Eventually a sac of reproductive parts of the parasite appears under the

tail of the female crab. If it is dangerous for the host to have a soft shell, it is equally dangerous for the parasite. So the growth of the parasitic barnacle inhibits any change of shell by the host. After the parasite has released sperm or ova into the sea it dies and the crab at once reverts to its normal rhythm of life.

'Here we have a much smaller, rounder crab, one with long antennae and with its flat nippers and body covered with fine hairs. This is the Broad-clawed Porcelain, *Porcellana platycheles*. They are about half an inch (12 millimetres) across and common under stones, where the hairs help to secure them into the muddy sand. They do not catch food with their nippers but, instead, they fish for it by casting out a sticky, web-fine net from their mouth to which the planktonic food adheres as they suck the net in again.

'Whereas crabs have ten legs, including the nippers, the porcelains appear to have only eight. The last pair are there, but are folded under the tail and have become part of the crab's reproductive apparatus. This position of the back legs indicates the relationship of these porcelains with the hermits and lobsters.

'Crabs are well adapted to survive the hazard of having legs trapped under stones rolled on them during storms. Unless it can escape from this trap, the crab will soon starve. The trapped leg (or legs) can be broken off across a groove in its second

80

joint by a specialised muscular contraction. In the residual stump are two membranous flaps which unfold as the leg is sheared and so staunch the flow of blood, the first drops of which, quickly coagulate and so totally seal the outlet. Then a complete new limb develops so fast within the stump that, a few weeks later, at the next change of shell, the leg emerges almost full size. Several legs can be replaced at this speed, at the same time.

'The ability to replace damaged parts, characteristic particularly of crustacea and starfish, reaches its climax with self-evisceration by sea-cucumbers. At the critical moment of attack by a predator, by a convulsive body contraction, the sea-cucumber causes its own gut to rupture and its viscera, genital organs and respiratory tissue are squirted out through its anus. This mass is strangely elastic and sticky and, at once, swells out into a white ball of 'cotton'. (Hence the vernacular name Cotton-spinners for sea-cucumbers.) The predator is distracted from the remaining body within which a new set of guts grows within ten days.'

As our search progressed we noticed that a number of seaweeds were peppered with little white dots which on inspection through a handlens turned out to be spirals. What were these?

'They are tubes within which worms live. There are not many worms on a rocky shore; they cannot burrow into rocks for shelter. However, two are easy to find. Both

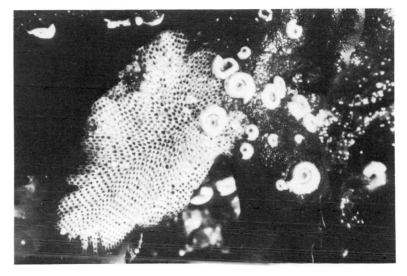

The rectangular tracery of a small patch of the sea-mat, *Membranipora membranacea* and tube worms, *Spirorbis borealis,* spired clockwise and having ridges along their length.

are able to extract molecules of calcium carbonate from the seawater from which they build stone-hard white tubes, within which they live in safety. The one we are looking at now is often on Bladder and Saw Wrack. Inside each spiral is a worm called *Spirorbis*. It is hermaphrodite and so fertilizes its own eggs, leading to larvae which swim away into the plankton. When they settle back as minute adults, no bigger than a pin head, they save themselves from at once being washed away, by seeking the shelter under the ridge of the midrib of these wracks. None that settles actually on the midrib, survives.

'The other white tube worm you will find is *Pomatoceros*. Its tube is much bigger than *Spirorbis*. Although built in the same way, it

The orange globular colonies of a sea-squirt low down on a rocky shore. Within each colony are ten to fifteen individual animals. Sea-squirts (*tunicates*) have tadpole-like larvae whose bodies are stiffened by a cartilaginous thread which is lost when they change into adults and which echo the evolutionary appearance of a backbone some 420 million years ago. In the middle of the picture, the open crown of tentacles of

is triangular in cross-section. At the open end of the tube a tiny needle growth point indicates that an animal is alive within. *Pomatoceros* is often found on small flat stones, usually several together.

'You may also find some scale worms under stones. These have interlocking pairs of scales protecting their backs. They progress by sideways wriggling.'

We just had time left before the tide turned to go still lower down into gullies between the rocks. They abounded with red seaweeds and the large oarweeds, *Laminaria* species.

'Down here, particularly under the rock overhangs, you will easily find lovely patches of bright colours – often orange or green. These are sponges. Thirty species of these primitive animals flourish on our rocky shores. Through a lens you can sometimes make out the tiny hole through which the animal draws in seawater – once again, for oxygen and food. Their waste is expelled through communal 'drains' which look like miniature volcanoes. These outlets are particularly prominent on a lump of Breadcrumb sponge, *Halichondria panicea*, less so on the other very common species, *Hymeni-*

acidon sanguinea. (Anybody who grows Chrysanthemum, Alstromeria or Antirrhinum in his garden has no reason to shy at the name *Hymeniacidon!*)

'If you look at the stalks of the oarweeds and many of the Saw Wracks at this level, you will see that they are wrapped round by a grey encrustation. On the oarweed fronds are irregular patches of the same kind of material. Through a hand lens you will see that each is made up of a fine honeycomb of tiny cells, regularly shaped. In each of these cells lives an animal, a Sea Mat. The two scientific names for the phylum, which contains them, suggests something of their character – Polyzoa, many animals, and Bryozoa, moss animals.

'Besides being so common, Sea Mats are complicated. They have a mouth leading into a digestive tract which curls up to an anus situated outside the circlet of tentacles on which fine hairs beat a stream of water into the central mouth. Each animal within its cell is a single entity. The corporate colony spreads and fuses where two edges of it meet. However, no fusion follows the meeting of separate colonies of the same species.

a tube-worm is extended for feeding beyond the grey end of its tube.

Left **Tubes of the worm,** *Pomatoceros triqueter*; the needle-sharp points over the open end of the left-hand three indicate the worm inside each is alive.

Below **Common sponges: the green form of the Breadcrumb Sponge** (*Halichondria panicea*), **mixed with orange pieces of** *Hymeniacidon sanguinea.*

'Commonly growing on these Sea Mat colonies, or on the seaweeds or the rocks, are little straw-coloured stalks, half an inch (12 millimetres) or more long. Through your lens you find that some have stubby pairs of lateral branches and some diaphanous divisions of the stem. These are colonies of sea-firs (hydroids), related to sea anemones and jellyfish. Within each cup, spaced along the branches, is a living animal surmounted by tentacles round its central mouth/anus. The beauty of the rhythmical beating of these tentacles has to be seen to be believed.'

There were so many other things to see but we had no time left. The competition for a place to live low down on rocky shores excludes all but fragmentary views of the underlying rock. Plants and animals are one on another – *Spirorbis*, hydroids, Sea Mats and other red seaweeds all cling on to Saw Wrack; barnacles and seaweeds are growing on limpets. Every nook and cranny is occupied. The variety of species and the beauty of their colours, patterns and movements will bring joy to any naturalist, and above all, to those with a seeing eye.

Now the flood tide was pushing us inexorably upwards. We had hardly covered more than a hundred yards since we started and had, even so, no more than glimpsed the riches that were before us on this length of rocky shore in Pembrokeshire.

The open network of thread 'rootlets' supporting a colony of the sea-fir (hydroid) *Dynamena pumila*, with cups in closely opposite pairs, in each of which lives a minute sea-anemone-like animal.

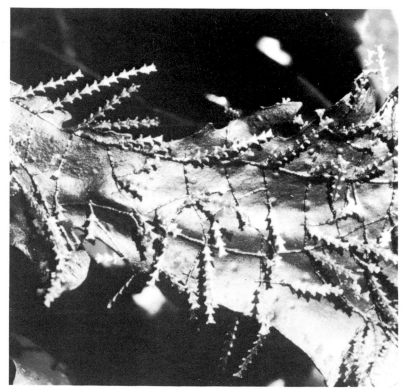

Shingle Beaches

If you are a holiday maker you might not have anything good to say for shingle beaches; they are pretty hard going on the feet, and you would think that they would be devoid of interest even for an enthusiastic natural historian. But you would be quite wrong. In this chapter, Ian Mercer takes us for a stroll across the shingle at Slapton in Devon and shows us just how fascinating they can be.

I remember first meeting Ian Mercer when he was a Field Assistant at Juniper Hall Field Centre in Surrey. He is the only man I know who can be enthusiastic about taking meteorological readings in the pouring rain. Since that time he has developed a special expertise on the environment at Slapton Ley, having run the field centre there for ten years.

The Yellow-horned Poppy (*Glacium flavum***), one of our most attractive seaside plants with its bright yellow flowers and long twisting seed pods.**

Information

Shingle beaches are characteristic of depositional coasts and are composed mainly of marine eroded pebbles. The most common type of shingle beach is one that simply fringes the coast, as along the Sussex coast. These are caused by the sorting action of the waves leaving the heavier pebbles at the top of the shore and finer materials further down. The action of longshore drift (see page 105) and offshore currents as well as outflow from rivers can combine to form spectacular shingle spits and bars. Often these formations are highly complex, showing successive periods of growth and retreat. The most well-known is the extensive bar of Chesil Beach. Other famous examples are found particularly on the North Sea coast. Where a shingle spit is formed across a bay it will sometimes develop so as to completely cut off the bay itself. The trapped water will then either form a brackish water lagoon or if it is fed by a river and becomes completely cut off, it will form a freshwater lake, as at Slapton Ley in Devon.

Although shingle beaches do not suffer from wind erosion in the same way as the upper reaches of sandy beaches they are still extremely unstable, particularly below the high spring water mark. The whole beach profile can change overnight if it is subjected to a heavy storm or an exceptionally high spring tide. Because of this constant resorting of the pebbles, the foreshore is generally barren of life and it is not until the upper shore that any colonisation by plants begins. However, once this has started the succession is quite rapid. The diagram shows some of the key plants in the development of the shingle beach flora. It must be remembered that each beach has its own topography and therefore some stages may be more pronounced, whilst other stages may be very much reduced or missing altogether.

Plant succession on a shingle ridge

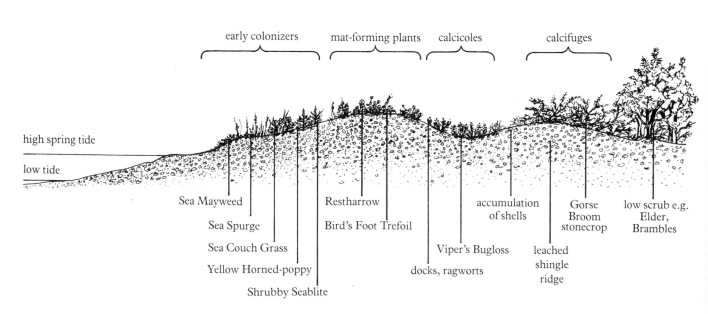

Some plants and animals to look out for:

Plants

Early colonisers:

Sea Kale *Crambe maritima*
Yellow Horned-poppy *Glaucium flavum*
Sea Sandwort *Honkenya peploides*
Sea Holly *Eryngium maritmum*
Sea Mayweed *Tripleurosermum maritimum*
Sea Pea *Lathyrus japonicus*
Sea Spurge *Euphorbia paralias*
Shrubby Seablite *Suaeda fruticosa*
Sea Couch Grass *Agropyron junceiforme*
Curled Dock *Rumex crispus* var. *trianulatus*

Fixed shingle:

Sea Radish *Raphanus raphanistrum*
   ssp. *maritimus*
Sea Campion *Silene maritima*
Sea Bindweed *Calstegia soldanella*
Restharrow *Ononis repens*
Birdsfoot Trefoil *Lotus corniculatus*
Kidney Vetch *Anthyllis vulneraria*
Ragwort *Senecio jacobaea*
Herb Robert *Geranium robertianum*
Viper's Bugloss *Echium vulgare*
Sea Carrot *Daucus carota*

Birds

Oystercatcher *Haematopus ostralegus*
Turnstone *Arenaria interpres*
Ringed Plover *Charadrius hiaticula*
Common Tern *Sterna hirundo*
Sandwich Tern *Sterna sandvicensis*
Little Tern *Sterna albifrons*

Sites

The following is a selection of shingle bars and spits from around our coasts. The beaches of South and East England are frequently fringed with shingle on the upper shore. Because of the unstable nature of shingle, some of these sites are particularly prone to erosion from trampling. Also certain more isolated stretches may have nesting birds, so make sure that it is all right to walk over them first, particularly in spring.

Culbin Sands, Grampian. An area of shingle and sand bars, including some lagoons. The mainland is heavily forested.

Spurn Point, Humberside. A three-mile spit which has developed on the north side of the Humber estuary. Local Nature Reserve with a bird observatory at the point.

Scolt Head, Norfolk. National Nature Reserve. A fascinating area of saltmarsh and shingle with good botanic and birdwatching interest. It is important to avoid the terneries in spring.

Blakeney Point, Norfolk. National Trust. Extensive area of shingle with interesting plants. Mostly maintained as a bird sanctuary as there are large colonies of nesting birds.

Orfordness, Suffolk. Vast area of shingle – one of the largest spits in the country – diverting the Alde eleven miles southward. Interesting shingle plants to be seen.

Dungeness, Kent. Prominent coastal headland developed by successive beaches. Good birdwatching as well as interesting flora.

Hurst Point, Hampshire. A four-mile shingle spit stretching out towards the Isle of Wight, with Hurst Castle at its tip.

Chesil Beach, Dorset. Famous shingle beach forming an eighteen-mile bar from Portland in the east to Bridport and also enclosing the extensive Fleet lagoon. The beach is unusually high in places, reaching up to 10 metres, with extensive areas of Shrubby Seablite on the landward side.

Slapton Sands, Devon. Shingle beach enclosing Slapton Ley. Field Studies Centre at Slapton village.

Shingle Beaches
with Ian Mercer

All too often when you are down at the seaside and you think you've found a nice sandy beach you discover that is made up of medium-sized rounded pebbles that grind away under your feet and are certainly no good for making sand castles! These beaches, with their great drifts of pebbles, often appear devoid of life, yet even here there are a few hardy plants that have established a foothold. There are classic shingle beaches throughout Britain, for example those found along the great depositional stretches of the East Anglian coast, but one of the most famous must be the great sweep of Chesil Beach between the Isle of Portland and Bridport, on the Dorset coast. Chesil has a smaller sister beach, Slapton Sands, which is at the opposite end of the huge bay that runs from Portland Bill round to Start Point. In order to find out more about the

formation of these beaches and their wildlife, we went down through the heart of holiday Devon to Slapton to meet Ian Mercer, who was to be our guide. Ian Mercer was a warden for the Field Studies Council, who founded and ran Slapton Ley Field Centre for ten years. He is now Chairman of the Field Studies Council and is Dartmoor National Park Officer by profession.

We started our walk on a hot July day appropriately down by the edge of the sea, having carefully picked our way through the sunbathing holidaymakers. I asked Ian to introduce us to the overall geography of the site.

'We're standing at about the middle of Slapton Sands, which at high tide stretches for some three miles from Torcross in the south to Pilchard Cove in the north. At low

A bird's-eye view of Slapton Sands with Slapton Ley to the right. This shingle bar is still slowly moving inland gradually filling in the ley (lake).

water, it is part of a 7 mile strip of shingle that ends at Hallsands. If you can picture a map of the Channel coast, we are actually at one end of a very big bay, with Chesil Beach and Portland Bill at the other end. These shingle beaches are at either end of the bay, and in between them are sandy beaches and cliffs, except where pebbles are provided by local cliffs or rivers. Only 20000 years ago, the coastline was more or less a straight line between Start Point and Portland Bill, but since then the sea level has risen, creating the present coastline.

'This shingle beach was, until recently, thought to have started life as a spit which gradually grew out from the north end of Start Bay, eventually cutting off the fresh-water outflow at Torcross and so creating the lagoon of Slapton Ley which is behind the beach. During the Nineteenth Century, there was a continuous outflow of fresh water at the southern end of the beach in winter. This water came from the River Gara, whose waters flowed into the bay at its northern end and which was then diverted southwards by the supposedly extending spit. But more and more evidence points to the fact that the whole beach actually came inland as one barrier being swept in front of a rising sea level. Today this ridge is still being washed inland and the Ley behind is slowly being squashed against the old cliffs. The Ley was thus once bigger and we have found that after a decent gale which can whip all the shingle off the front, you find traces of peat and clay layers which are the old floor of the lake. So the shingle is really travelling over the lake bed. What we are looking at is, in fact, a very recent mobile landscape.

'Most of the pebbles you can see on the beach have been picked up by the sea during its rise. The overall colour of the beach is an orange-fawn; this is because the dominant pebbles are these brownish weathered and eroded flints. There isn't any chalk any-where on the coastline now, so these pebbles have been actually swept up from the chalk that is in the bed of the English Channel. The second most common pebble is the quartz, which is white. Chemically, the flint and the quartz are almost identical, and they are both very hard, which is why so many of them have survived for so long. I suppose they average a centimetre or less in diameter, although it is obviously the bigger ones that catch your eye. All the other colours, which are less dominant, are the local stones. They are either from the cliffs that you can see at either end of the bay or

Most of the pebbles making up the shingle are weathered flints and quartz, made smooth and round by constantly grinding against each other under the force of the waves and sea currents.

The shingle beach is steeply shelving due to 'washback' from the receding waves. The larger pebbles are left along the high tide mark as they are heavier than the smaller ones. This photograph shows how empty a shingle beach can be. The constant movement of the pebbles means that it is difficult for organisms to survive. It is difficult enough walking on the pebbles, so just think of the problems of living there!

250 miles from the Straits of Dover. The waves from the south-west, which everybody would expect to be the dominant direction as it is, of course, that of the prevailing wind, have to come round that corner, Start Point, to arrive here and in doing so they lose all their energy.

'Also you will notice that the shingle is zoned at each high water mark. When you can see a series of decreasing ridges like this, you know that you are in a series of neap tides. When the next spring tide comes along it will wash all these away and the beach will have a more uniform profile. If you look here, where we had the last high tide mark, you can see that the pebbles have sorted themselves out, with the large ones being left behind. The local slates and thin sandstones skate over the little round pebbles – almost as if they were moving on rollers – and you tend to find them accumulating in pockets.'

Compared with the rocky shoreline we had looked at last month, it was very barren. I asked Ian if there was any life at all down here at the water's edge.

'It is very sterile from a marine point of view, and you have to go well offshore before you find anything alive simply because it is all so mobile. There are patches of kelp washed up on the strand line, but the main life here is holidaymakers and roosting gulls. These gulls seem to spend most of their time just standing around. They feed offshore and inland following the plough. They are, of course, great opportunists, and feed on the litter bins and on what people throw to them. But if a tractor starts up, sometimes you will see them all fly up and go to see what the farmer is doing. They like the open beach as it gives them a clear view of any approaching danger. Interestingly, they appear to zone themselves, with the larger Greater Black-backed Gulls at the bottom by the water's edge, the Herring Gulls in the middle, and the Black-headed Gulls at the top which can presumably take off the fastest.

'In the spring and autumn, there are huge passages of birds along this coast. In the spring, a lot of the birds come in over Start Point and then work up the coast; in the autumn, there is a great movement down Channel along the English coastline, and they turn here to go south over to France. Start Point is a great take-off point for these migratory birds, so we have a lot of terns and various other seabirds passing through.'

they have come down rivers, like the Dart, and contain rocks like granite, slates and sandstones.

'The most important thing about the shingle from the point of view of its zonation and the life that it can support, is that it is incredibly mobile. The wind is north of east at the moment, and therefore today waves are drifting this shingle slowly southwards. You will notice here that if you walk down the length of the beach from north to south the pebble size becomes more coarse. This is because the larger pebbles are washed that way on more days than the other way. When weaker waves are running from the south some of the smaller stones may be washed northwards, but the larger ones are left behind. The biggest waves on this beach come from just north of east down the Channel as they have a straight run of about

A flock of Herring Gulls taking off down the beach. These gulls use the open beach as a roost where they can easily detect any approaching danger.

We turned landward, and made our way across the pebbly ridges towards the more fixed stretches of shingle above extreme high water mark. At one point, we came upon a large patch of weathered shells in a hollow. They were mostly broken cockle shells; later we were to see how these accumulations affect the plant life further inland.

We had hardly walked more than fifteen metres before we started to find the first of the pioneer plants. Ian described them:

'We have now reached a zone where the shingle is more stable, although a strong gale will certainly wash the pebbles away up this far. Over to our right, you can see that part of this ridge has been eaten into by a recent gale, so this is still a fairly precarious area and still obviously mobile. Yet here we have some flowering plants which are obviously doing well. This first one here is the Sea Mayweed, *Tripleurospermum maritimum*, which has a white daisy-like flower and these finely divided leaves. It looks like a more fleshy version of the Scentless Mayweed, which is a common weed on disturbed ground inland. Now, apart from having to contend with the movement of the pebbles, the main problem facing these colonizers is drought. These pebbles are not bound together with any soil or humus here, so any rain will just drain straight through. The Sea Mayweed's main adaptation to this is to have a very long root system which reaches a point where the pebbles are so cold that

One of the first colonisers of the beach – Sea Mayweed (*Tripleurospermum maritimum*). This plant has a very long root system which enables it to reach the water formed by condensation deep in the shingle.

the vapour in the air condenses, forming an underground dew. There is also a fresh-water table down in the shingle, because the surface of Slapton Ley is perched above the sea level and consequently there is always water seeping through the shingle bank into the sea. So, if the plants have long enough roots they will be well on the way to surviving. Another plant that is out here is the Curled Dock, *Rumex crispus*, which is really an arable weed, but in the same way that it manages to take advantage of disturbed ground inland with its wind blown seeds and long tap root, it also does well here, enjoying the lack of competition that this otherwise inhospitable situation gives it.

'Over here is an interesting plant of this pioneer zone – the Sea Spurge, *Euphorbia paralias*. This is a member of the ubiquitous spurge family that seems to have a member

93

adapted for every situation you can think of. This is a small, almost succulent, plant with a very elaborate flower – green petals and a little yellow centre. The plant itself, like a Dandelion, is full of latex. The colour of the plant is a pale blue-green; this is caused by a fine covering of hairs over the leaves, and is another adaptation against water loss. Its low squat habit also means that the winds that whip over here do not cause too much water loss. But despite its short appearance – and the plants here are all under fifteen centimetres in height – it has, like the docks, an extensive root system. When I used to teach here at the Field Centre and before

there were protective laws, we would send out the occasional recalcitrant student to bring back the root system intact. They would be rather dismayed when they found out that this tiny plant has roots that go down over two metres.

'Next to it here is a grass, again with this same colour – dusty blue-green – as a result of the fine covering of hairs. This is Sea Couch Grass, *Agropyron juncieforme*, which has extensive rhizomes which begin to bind the shingle together. Like the others it also obtains its moisture from the internal dew in the shingle. Sea Couch is very salt tolerant and grows much nearer the sea than the

Sea Spurge (*Euphorbia paralias*), like all members of the spurge family, bleeds white latex when broken. But please do not damage it in anyway, these plants of the pebbles are having a tough enough time already without us botanists adding to their problems.

Curled Dock (*Rumex crispus*), growing on the shingle beach ridge. Many of those red-brown fruits will fall on stony ground but a few will germinate and grow helping to stabilise the shingle.

other grasses. These perennials, such as the Sea Spurge and this couch, are very important in that they provide the stability which allows other plants to move in. Another plant here which is very noticeable, but is a biennial and so does not contribute as much to this colonization, is the Yellow Horned-poppy, *Glaucium flavum*. This starts off typically as a tight rosette of leaves, with these finer hairs over them, in its first year. In its second year the flower stalk pushes up and these showy yellow flowers are formed. It is called "horned" poppy because of the seed pods, which are unusual for a poppy in that they are very long and thin, up to thirty centimetres. When they dry out they twist, giving the appearance of a ram's horn.

'Now moving past these pioneers, we come to an area where the shingle is more stable and we start to find some important mat-forming plants. Down here, we have one of the more successful ones – Restharrow, *Ononis repens*. As its name implies, it is also a weed of arable land. The story goes that its densely matted stems would slow up the progress of the old harrows through the soil. It is a member of the pea family and has these characteristic pea-like flowers. If you feel it, the leaves are just slightly sticky and there are even gulls' feathers trapped on them

A mat of Restharrow (*Ononis repens*) **spreading its stabilising influence and providing a refuge for some fescue grasses and Wild Carrot** (*Daucus carota*).

A perfectly camouflaged wolf spider on the shingle.

The common or garden (or meadow, or mountain or seaside!) Yarrow (*Achillea millefolium*). A very plastic plant by nature, changing its growth form to suit its environment. Here, on the shingle, it is mat-forming.

Opposite left **Sea Radish** (*Raphanus raphanistrum* **ssp.** *maritimus*) **is a taller relative of the Wild Radish with bright yellow flowers. It is restricted to our south and west coasts. Wild Radish has long seed pods with up to eight seeds, whereas the Sea Radish only has two or three.**

here. This stickiness is very important because it traps other wind blown seeds, and if you look at this next patch you can see that it has other plants growing in the middle of it. So the Restharrow not only furthers the stabilization of the shingle by beginning to provide a continuous surface, but it then traps the next phase of plants in the succession. Here we can see some Red Fescue that has taken advantage of the little bit of humus that the dead Restharrow roots and leaves have provided.

'In fact, we are actually starting to see a soil forming here. Eventually, providing a great wave doesn't sweep up the beach and cover everything with a new layer of shingle, you will find that the patches of the mat-forming plants will amalgamate and some

less hardy plants will move in. Two other plants to look out for that have this same ability to form mats are the Bird's Foot Trefoil, *Lotus corniculatus*, and the Sea Bindweed, *Calystegia soldanella*. This bindweed has a far reaching system of rhizomes and, unlike its inland cousins, it does not climb but forms a sprawling mat over the shingle. Over here there is a clump of Bird's Foot Trefoil which is now dying back, but you can see that it has done its job because the centre of the patch is now dominated by fescue grass which will eventually take over completely from the trefoil.'

We were now only some ten metres from the first intrepid mayweeds and spurges, and yet all around new plants were coming in – Yarrow, various plantains and knapweeds. We were in a slight hollow, and Ian pointed out that there was probably an accumulation of shells under the soil which meant that there were a number of lime-loving plants to be seen – Wild Carrot and the feathery heads of Kidney Vetch. The dominant plant in this zone, though, was the tall yellow-flowered Sea Radish – a subspecies of the Wild Radish, *Raphanus raphanistrum* ssp. *maritimus*. Ian described it.

'This plant always reminds me of Slapton as it dominates this part of the shingle and hangs over the road which runs along the centre of the ridge, forming a yellow screen on either side. It starts off as a little rosette of leaves, probably as an adaptation against the wind, then it shoots up and in July it can be two metres high, topped by these typical yellow cabbage-type flowers with four petals. You can tell this one from the common Wild Radish as the fruit normally has two, sometimes three, seeds, whereas the Wild Radish has a long pod with up to eight seeds.

'Along the road here are a lot of typical roadside weeds, such as Mugwort, more docks and some hogweed. If we cross over the road, we will find what is actually another ridge of the shingle, although it is now cut off from the sea by the road. This older shingle shows some interesting properties associated with the degree of leaching in the soil.'

We made our way over the road and through the tangle of Sea Radish. As we came out on to a more open patch where the shingle was still visible, Ian pointed out some Broomrape – a parasitic plant with no chlorophyll of its own. This particular plant was probably attached to the roots of the Restharrow which is able to fix nitrogen from the soil and therefore makes an ideal host for these parasitic plants. This second ridge was very much more overgrown. However, Ian explained that this had happened only recently.

'One reason why it is so thick here is because there are no longer any Rabbits to keep it down. Until the 1950's, this area was a closely cropped sward and local farmers actually turned out their livestock to graze here, but since the outbreak of myxamotosis the Rabbits have retreated inland.

'We are on this second ridge, and you can see that it has some peculiar properties as a substrate for plant life because stretches have all the indications that it is acidic yet

Above **Unlike its countryside and urban cousins, the Sea Bindweed** (*Calystegia soldanella*) **does not climb but crawls and creeps about, binding the shingle.**

Left **Thrift** (*Armeria maritima*), **one of the most characteristic plants of the seaside. Its massed pink flowers make any sea-scape perfect.**

Above **Sea Campion**
(*Silene maritima*),
**another stabilising
influence on the shore.
It is closely related to
the Bladder Campion
(*S. vulgaris*) and
fertile hybrids can be
raised with ease,
although they are very
rare in nature.**

Right **Viper's Bugloss**
(*Echium vulgare*). **Its
bright blue spikes of
flowers are a sign of
calcium (resulting
from a hidden
accumulation of
shells) in the develop-
ing soil of a more
stable dune on the
landward side of the
shingle ridge.**

A natural pasture
blooming where once
the sea pounded the
pebbles.

elsewhere it is obviously lime-rich. The
reason for this is that the rain has been
leaching the shingle here longer than on the
new ridges, and so most of the mineral
nutrients have been washed down. If we
look around we can see acid-indicators like
this Sheep's Sorrel, *Rumex acetosella*, with
these leaves that I like to think look like a
medieval halberd, with those little spikes at
the base. This is a member of the dock
family, and is a coloniser of acid sites. Over
here, we have an even clearer indication of
the acid substrate – gorse. This is not the
common Gorse, *Ulex europaeus*, but is the
Western Gorse, *Ulex gallii*. It grows very
close to the ground in cushions, and flowers
late in the summer right through to
November, whereas *Ulex europaeus* flowers
mostly during the spring but also sporadic-
ally all the year round. You know the old
saying that when gorse is not in flower
kissing is out of fashion! There is also
Stonecrop here – again a plant which can
grow in these heavily leached and arid
conditions. It has almost the flora of an old
acid sand dune – the botanists call them
'grey' dunes because of the covering of
lichens, as opposed to the open 'yellow'
dunes where the Marram Grass grows.

'Intriguingly, having just described all
these acid-tolerant plants, if we look over
there we can see the handsome blue spikes
of Viper's Bugloss, which is a limestone
plant. Now what this means is that under
the thin layer of soil must be an accumulation of shells within the shingle, providing
the necessary calcium carbonate at that
point. So we get this strange mosaic, with
acid patches where everything is short and
surviving by the skin of its teeth, then only a
few metres away all the evident richness.
This occurs all along the ridge – you have a
patch of Bracken and Bluebells, indicating
acidic conditions, and you move on and you
are brushing against clematis and you're
back with lime-loving plants.

'Over here is a plant of this older shingle,

Elder. In front of us was the reed-fringed lagoon which the shingle bar had helped to form. Suddenly we were in a different world with reedmace and Purple Loosestrife growing along the edges next to us. This was Slapton Ley ('ley' is an Old English word for lake) and it would have been originally part of the bay but was now a rich freshwater lake. In fact, it is famous for its pike and Edward VII used to come here for the fishing.

We had not travelled more than 200 metres but had seen how the plant life had managed to fill almost every available niche. It had certainly shown that even the smallest potential for life was likely to be seized upon and exploited to the full. So next time you are down on one of our many shingle beaches see if you can piece together how the plants have managed to move in.

The top of the back ridge of the shingle. Here the rains have leached the soil and acid conditions prevail only metres from the pockets of calcium rich soil. This patch of shingle is dominated by acid-loving plants, such as Western Gorse (*Ulex gallii*), with the spent flowering spike of a Foxglove towering over it.

namely ragwort. This plant is a prolific coloniser of these sites. Looking inland, we can see that the plant cover becomes even thicker and we have things like Bracken and Brambles growing. Then behind those we have the final stage in this colonisation of the shingle – shrubs. Here are mostly Elder bushes and Sycamores up to four metres high. They are kept low by the wind which tends to kill back the more exposed buds. Nevertheless, they are now well established. Also, they do add a new element to the habitat and you have birds like Robins and Dunnocks, with the occasional Stonechat breeding in them. There may be even Grasshopper Warblers in there during a good year. However, by and large it is a pretty public place so that the more nervous birds do not tend to stay for very long.

'We have now seen a clear succession of plants up from the sea – the pioneer plants on the open shingle, through to patches of mat-forming plants gradually amalgamating to form a turf, which then becomes rank and leggy, eventually going into Brambles and, finally, into a zone of shrubs and low trees. There the development stops rather abruptly and if we make our way through some of this Bracken, we can see why.'

We pushed our way in between the dense herbage and arrived eventually under a low

Sand Dunes

A supply of readily erodible rock out to sea and an onshore wind means that the coast will be fringed and protected by a belt of sand dunes. The dunes themselves owe their continued existence to a whole group of hardy plants, the most important being two grasses: Marram and Sea Couch Grass. This environment is highly unstable and a strong gale can change the whole appearance of a mobile dune system overnight. Yet these support a complex web of life which has adapted to exploit the full potential of this transient and exciting landscape.

What better person than Ted Smith, whose inspiration helped found the county trust movement, which is now under the 'umbrella' of the Royal Society for Nature Conservation, to show us around the dunes at Gibraltar Point in Lincolnshire.

Lyme Grass (*Elymus arenarius*), **a distinctive plant of the open sand dunes of our coasts.**

Sand Dunes

Sand on the upper reaches of our sandy beaches is highly susceptible to movement by wind. On a dry sunny day, as any holiday-maker will tell you, vast amounts of sand are blown across the open beaches. When this reaches an obstruction, whether natural or man-made, the sand will start to accumulate, forming mini-dunes. The first area where this happens is usually at the high water mark strand line. Here the first of the plants will start to colonise the sand. As they consolidate it the sand becomes higher and, if there is a continuing supply of fresh sand, considerable dunes bound by thousands of Marram plants will form. The dunes will continue to rise, as the Marram Grass has the ability to grow up through successive coverings until eventually the wind speed and the angle of the dune are such that the sand will no longer accumulate. These dunes, however, are still mobile and susceptible to periodic 'blow-outs' caused by heavy storms or freak spring tides. Parallel ridges of dunes are often formed as the overall coastline continues to

Some plants and animals to look out for:

Plants

Foreshore:
Sea Rocket *Cakile maritima*
Prickly Saltwort *Salsola kali*
Sea Sandwort *Honkenya peploides*
Halberd-leaved Orache *Atriplex hastata*
Grass-leaved Orache *Atriplex littoralis*
Sea Couch Grass *Agropyron junceifirne*

Mobile/Yellow Dunes:
Lyme Grass *Elymus arenarius*
Marram Grass *Ammophila arenaria*
Red Fescue *Festuca rubra* var. *arenaria*
Sand Sedge *Carex arenaria*
Sea Holly *Eryngium maritimum*
Sea Bindweed *Calystegia soldanella*
Prickly Lettuce *Lactuca saligna*

Sea Spurge *Euphorbia paralias*
Sea Beet *Beta maritima*

Fixed/Grey Dunes:
Ragwort *Senecio jacobaea*
Scarlet Pimpernel *Anagallis arvensis*
Ladies' Bedstraw *Galium verum*
Viper's Bugloss *Echium vulgare*
Elder *Sambucus nigra*
Burnet Rose *Rosa pimpinellifolia*
Dewberry *Rosa caesius*
Sea Buckthorn *Hippophae rhamnoides*
Peltigera lichens
Cladonia lichens
Tortula ruraliformis moss
Many plants more typical of chalklands can often be found in the dune 'slacks'

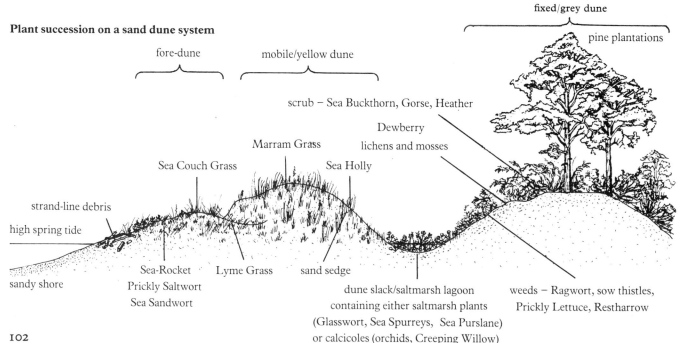

Plant succession on a sand dune system

fixed/grey dune

pine plantations

fore-dune

mobile/yellow dune

scrub – Sea Buckthorn, Gorse, Heather

Dewberry

lichens and mosses

Marram Grass

Sea Couch Grass

Sea Holly

strand-line debris

high spring tide

sandy shore

Sea-Rocket
Prickly Saltwort
Sea Sandwort

Lyme Grass

sand sedge

dune slack/saltmarsh lagoon
containing either saltmarsh plants
(Glasswort, Sea Spurreys, Sea Purslane)
or calcicoles (orchids, Creeping Willow)

weeds – Ragwort, sow thistles,
Prickly Lettuce, Restharrow

build and off-shore bars become incorporated into the mainland coast.

The plant development on these dunes can be very distinct with different species tending to colonise the various stages of the dune formation, as shown in the diagram. The older stages of the dunes can be dominated by dune scrub, characterised on the East Coast by Sea Buckthorn, or it can develop into dune heath, as at Studland Bay in Dorset. These dune heaths often support a rich fauna, including some of the rarer reptiles and amphibians. The general dune development can often be truncated by the delibrate planting of conifers or the creation of car parks and extensive golf courses.

Invertebrates

The high calcium content of certain mobile dunes means that they support large numbers of snails such as *Helicella*, *Helix*, *Cepaea* and *Cochlicella*.

Sandhopper *Talitrus saltator* – on strand line
Insects include many species associated with sandy heaths. Noticeable are:
Silver Y Moth *Autographa gamma*
Scarlet Tiger *Callimorpha dominula*
Cinnabar Moth *Tyria jacobaeae*
Robber flies *Asilus* spp.
Sand wasps *Ammophila* spp.
Green Tiger Beetle *Cicindela campestris*

Birds

Kestrel *Falco tinnunculus*
Turnstone *Arenaria interpres*
Sanderling *Calidris alba*
Short-eared Owl *Asio flammeus*
Skylark *Alauda arvensis*
Shorelark *Eremophila alpestris*
Snow Bunting *Plectrophenax nivalis*

Mammals

Long-tailed Field Mouse *Apodemus sylvaticus*
Short-tailed Vole *Microtus agrestis*
Rabbit *Oryctolagus cuniculus*
Fox *Vulpes vulpes*

Sites

The following is a selection of some of the more interesting sand dune areas around our coasts. Some of these areas arc reserves and it is suggested that you consult one of the many regional guides before intending to visit any of them. Remember that sand dunes are an extremely unstable environment and can suffer from too much trampling, so always try to keep to recognised routes or nature trails.

Culbin Sands, Grampian. An area of shingle and sand bars, including some old ridges reaching 30 metres in height. The mainland is heavily forested.
Sands of Forvie, Grampian. National Nature Reserve. Extensive sand dune system with good plant succession leading to dune heath.
Tentsmuir Point, Fife. National Nature Reserve. Well-developed system of sand dunes with good plant succession leading to afforested dune heath.
Lindisfarne, Northumberland. National Nature Reserve. Large dune system on Holy Island and on the mainland at Ross Links. Superb area with a wide range of coastal habitats.
Gibraltar Point, Lincolnshire. Nature reserve managed by the Lincolnshire and South Humberside Naturalists' Trust. Area of dunes and saltmarsh with sand and shingle beaches. Bird observatory, see page 122.
North Norfolk Coast. Good areas of sand dunes all along the coast notably at Hunstanton, Holme, Scolt Head and areas of Blakeney Point.

Sandwich Bay, Kent. Area of sand dunes which is good for both flowers and bird life. RSPB, National Trust and Kent Trust for Nature Conservation joint reserve.
Studland Bay, Dorset. National Nature Reserve. Extensive area of dunes which have become stabilised to form dune heath. Good range of plants but noteworthy also for its fauna which include some of our rarer birds and reptiles.
Dawlish Warren, Devon. Local Nature Reserve. Area of sand dunes showing dune succession. Also good for bird watching across the estuary in winter
Braunton Burrows, Devon. National Nature Reserve. Most extensive sand dune system in the South West, with dunes reaching 30 metres in height. Occasionally used by the Ministry of Defence. Excellent dune flora and fauna.
Whiteford Burrows, Glamorgan. National Nature Reserve. Area of sand dunes and saltings. Good for both botanising and birdwatching. Worth visiting Oxwich Burrows on the south side of the Gower Peninsula, also a National Nature Reserve.
Cors Fochno, Dyfed. Nature Reserve. Coastal stretch has a good series of sand dunes with a duneland nature trail.
Newborough Warren, Gwynedd. National Nature Reserve. Extensive area of excellent dunes showing plant succession.
Ainsdale, Merseyside. National Nature Reserve. Large area of dunes showing succession through to pine plantation. Interesting fauna including rarer reptiles and amphibians.

Sand Dunes
with Ted Smith

A gently sloping beach backed by a rolling belt of dunes is many people's idea of the perfect place to be on a warm summer's day. I can always remember the feeling of excitement when, as a boy, we would set off through the dunes towards the sea, especially when we mounted that final crest and the wide sandy beach would suddenly open out before us. The waves would be breaking down by the water's edge and small flocks of gulls would be drifting along between the distant knots of sunbathers. Tremendous. But for a naturalist the walk through the dunes themselves is as exciting as the beach, as we found out during our visit to Gibraltar Point Nature Reserve. Our guide through the ups and downs of this unstable environment was Ted Smith, who is Chairman of the Lincolnshire and South Humberside Trust for Nature Conservation and also, until recently, was the General Secretary of the RSNC (then the Society for the Promotion of Nature Conservation). Ted has known the dunes at Gibraltar Point for many years and is all too aware of the changes they have undergone since the war, in terms of both public pressures and physical change. We started our walk down by the strand line and whilst we picked our way between the flotsam and jetsam Ted introduced us to the site.

'We are here on the Lincolnshire coast at the Gibraltar Point Nature Reserve which consists of a large area of sand dunes and saltmarsh with both sandy and muddy beaches. It is at the north-west corner of the Wash and on a clear day you can see the coast of Norfolk, 13 miles away. The reserve covers about 1 000 acres and has been established since 1949, making it one of the earliest post-war nature reserves. It is managed by the Lincolnshire and South Humberside Trust for Nature Conservation on behalf of the owners who are the Lincolnshire County Council and the East Lindsey District Council.

'Any walk among the sand dunes ought to start out on the beach and that is where we are now, looking out to sea on a beautiful summer day with the waves tumbling lazily on shore. But if we were to visit this coast at a time of a big storm or when a high spring tide was flowing, we would see that the waves would be driving the sand and shingle up the beach. Quite a lot of this material is washed back into the sea but some of it remains on the upper part of the beach. On some parts of the coast the waves

come in at a right angle to the shore but often they come in at an oblique angle carrying sand and shingle in that direction. Some of this material is then dragged back into the sea at a right angle to the waterline with the backwash, and in this way the sand and pebbles are gradually carried along the shore. This process is known as "beach drifting". Here, you can see long ridges being built up southwards indicating the direction in which the beach material is moving at this particular point.

'As the tides return to a succession of neaps, leaving much of the shore exposed for long periods, the sand will dry out and the wind then comes into play and blows it further inland. Anything that traps this moving sand will serve to build up the beach. The first thing that does this is the tide wrack along the strand line, which is at our feet. This includes all sorts of human rubbish but most of it is natural material – either dead plant remains from saltmarshes or remains that have been washed up from the seabed. On rocky coasts a great deal of this would be seaweeds but here a lot of the wrack is made up of this brown stuff that looks for all the world like dried-up brown seaweed but is, in fact, of animal origin. It is called Seamat or Hornwrack and it was once growing on the seabed, attached by little pads, then spreading out, like the fingers of a hand. If we look at this specimen under a lens you will see that it looks rather like a honeycomb pitted with tiny cells. Each cell, when it is alive, contains a minute animal that lives by drawing in tiny morsels from the sea. It is a colony of animals and belongs to a group called Polyzoa, meaning "many animals". These dried remnants which resemble tiny, tufted trees are called Sea Firs. They housed colonies of hydroids.

'There is a lot of other material here. It is all very dry at this time of year as some of it has been here since last winter's gales. These are whelks' egg-cases, the familiar papery brown clusters of little balls; and these shiny black objects with horns at each corner are skates' egg-cases – "mermaids' purses". From our point of view all this dead material is important because it is the first thing that traps the blowing sand. It will also eventually rot down, like garden compost, to provide nutrients for the first land plants to grow. Incidentally, it is also the home for many small animals, particularly sandhoppers, which live in burrows under the wrack and come out at night to

The strandline – the first stage in the accumulation of the sand. This photograph shows a typical collection of flotsam and jetsam – whelk egg-cases, 'mermaids' purses' (skates' eggs), hornwrack, sea firs and human debris.

large sprawling plant has pretty wallflower-like mauve flowers and, in fact, it belongs to the same family – the crucifers. It is an annual and, as you can see, by this time in the summer, it has really built up into quite a substantial clump. Its sprawling branches lying flat on the ground manage to collect quite a lot of sand and it has formed little dunes all along the beach here. It produces very abundant seed pods which are shaped rather like urns. They get washed out into the tide wrack and will be carried along the beach by the waves until they find a suitable niche where, next spring, the seeds can begin to grow. This is obviously a very chancy sort of existence and some summers there is very little Sea Rocket to be seen. This year, though, it is particularly abundant. It is a favourite plant for insects and you can see there are many bumblebees feeding on it. Another insect which you can find here is the Silver-Y Moth, which is a very pretty brown, black and purplish moth with a little silver "Y" on the forewing. The British population of this moth is entirely dependent on immigrants from the Continent in early summer which then breed here but do not overwinter.

'There is another early plant colonist on these dunes – here it is, this spiny-leaved plant, Prickly Saltwort, *Salsola kali*, which, like the Sea Rocket, you will find all around our coasts. It is also an annual and develops into a big rather sprawling bush by the end of the summer, helping to collect and consolidate its quota of sand. Typically these two plants grow together forming a zone along the upper strand line, as they do here. Obviously they must be able to tolerate quite a lot of salt because they are occasionally swamped by high tides and frequently subjected to spray drift. Saltwort like Glasswort, which we will meet later on, absorbs so much salt that it used to be burnt to provide soda for making soap and glass.

'Perhaps, at this point, we ought to ask ourselves a few more questions about the conditions in which some of these plants have to grow. It really is a most inhospitable habitat at first glance. For one thing, they don't have much soil to grow in, although they do derive some humus from the rotting debris on the strand line. But the main problem is one of insuring that they have enough water. As we can see, the surface layers of the sand are extremely dry. The rain falls and disappears almost immediately, but if we dig down a little way it begins to be moist,

Above the strandline one of the first flowering plants to colonise the dunes is Sea Rocket (*Cakile maritima*). This sprawling crucifer provides a bright splash of colour amongst all the sand. Behind it is a clump of Lyme Grass (*Elymus arenarius*), one of the important dune forming grasses.

feed. If we were to disturb this wrack in the cool of the evening they would go jumping away in their thousands. You might be lucky enough in autumn or winter to see a Sanderling, one of the smallest and most agile of our shorebirds, chasing these sandhoppers, or better still, the more ponderous Turnstone snapping them up after pulling over the wrack.

'Quite often the first plants found growing along the strand line on the upper beach deriving nourishment from the buried debris, are fungi. One of them, the fairy-cup, *Geopyxis ammophila*, appears as a pale brown sphere which gradually opens into a cup with its rim at the level of the sand. But it is the first of the flowering plants which catches our attention and here is a marvellous carpet of Sea Rocket, *Cakile maritima*, just to the landward side of the wrack. This

Prickly Saltwort
(*Salsola kali*), another
early coloniser. This
plant is able to
absorb so much salt it
used to be burnt to
provide soda for
making soap and
glass.

to adapt themselves in various ways to avoid losing too much moisture. Sea Rocket has fleshy leaves which contain a large amount of water. Prickly Saltwort has a narrow spine-like leaf, so it has a relatively small surface area through which moisture can be lost. Both of the plants here are also low-growing, forming a mat of branches and leaves near the surface. This means that less of the plant is exposed to the desiccating effect of the wind so a certain amount of moisture is conserved under the mass of leaves. Most of the dune plants we will be looking at have some kind of device for making sure that they don't lose too much water.

'In addition to the Sea Rocket and Prickly Saltwort there are a number of other plants that are able to grow in these very early stages of dune formation. This is one of them. It is a species of Orache, the Halberd-leaved Orache, *Atriplex hastata*, and there is another, the Grass-leaved Orache, *Atriplex littoralis*. They are rather undistinguished plants with small green flowers in spikes. Another plant which grows successfully out here is the Sea Sandwort, *Honkenya peploides*. It has glossy green, fleshy leaves which are arranged along the stem in opposite pairs, making it very pleasing to look at. Although only a very small plant, growing two or three inches high, you can see that it has managed to collect a very considerable mound of sand around it. Furthermore, it has the ability to continue to grow up after being covered, and here you can see these new shoots coming through the wind-blown sand.

so that if the plant has developed a fairly deep and extensive rooting system it can draw on moisture. But that is not the only moisture problem, because on a very dry, breezy and sunny day like this, the plant is drawing up moisture and losing it by evaporation from its leaves. We know that on a day like this in the garden, very often a plant will wilt simply because its supply of water at the roots is not keeping pace with the loss of moisture through its leaves. The plants here on the exposed shore, have had

An orache (*Atriplex spp*), one of the plants that has adapted to living in these arid conditions.

Sea Sandwort (*Honkenya peploides*). This pleasing plant with its regularly spaced succulent leaves has formed its own mini-sand dune. Its low creeping habit is an adaption to the desiccating effect of the wind.

'Although these plants are important in their own way, the real builders of the sand dunes are the grasses and, if we walk along the front of the dunes here, we will be able to see the three main species.'

We made our way along to an area where the dunes were rising steeply out from the beach, where the grasses were obviously the dominant plants. Ted described them.

'The first grass to build up these fore-dunes is the Sand Couch Grass, *Agropyron junceiforme*. It is a relative of the Couch or Twitch which is such a pest in some of our gardens. This grass has a very extensive rooting system, running by underground stems or rhizomes, and then pushing up aerial shoots at frequent intervals. Like many of the plants here, it has the ability to grow up through the sand when it has been covered over. But its ability to grow upwards is limited and so we have to look for more powerful grasses to increase the height of the dune, and two that do that pre-eminently are the Marram Grass, *Ammophila arenaria*, and the Lyme Grass, *Elymus arenarius*.

'The Lyme Grass is not such an abundant grass around the coast of Britain as the Marram. It is very striking, having a very distinctive colour – a blue-green on the upper side of the leaves, where it has these very prominent ribs and grooves. I spoke earlier about the devices for checking transpiration and, in these grasses, the stomata – the pores on the leaf through which moisture is lost – are mostly situated down in the grooves. Moreover, the grass ensures that they are further protected because in dry weather the leaf rolls up into a tube. This is especially noticeable in the Marram. Its appearance on a wet day, after rain, is quite different from that which we can see today, as the leaves would be open and flat.

'Along here the dune has been cliffed back by last winter's tides and it has exposed the rooting system of the Marram. Look at this tremendous mat of roots which not only helps to collect the sand but also binds and consolidates it. This little cliff shows that the Marram roots go down well over a metre or so and I have seen dunes with sections cut away to over two metres and the roots still go right down. Even at the bottom where they

Sea Couch Grass (*Agropyron junceiforme*). This grass is important in stabilising the fore-dunes, being able to continue to push shoots up through successive coverings of sand. But it is not as powerful as its relative – Marram Grass, which can be seen in the background.

This sand dune which has been 'cliffed' back by last winter's tides clearly shows the extensive rooting system of Marram Grass (*Ammophila arenaria*). This grass is instrumental in building great ridges of sand around our coasts, some of which reach over thirty metres in height.

are dead, they are still performing the function of holding the sand together. Marram dunes in this country grow to about 20–25 metres (60–70 feet), but on the Continent they can go much higher, reaching over 33 metres (100 feet) on the Baltic coasts. As long as mobile sand is available Marram will go on building dunes almost indefinitely, but to flourish it does need a constant supply of new sand. It was widely used, incidentally, in coastal areas in the past for weaving mats – hence the old name of mat grass – and also for thatching stacks and buildings. Its importance for consolidating dunes as a sea defence was also clearly recognised and in many places – as on the Lincolnshire coast here – it was forbidden to cut it as long ago as the Fourteenth Century.'

We then headed inland, making our way between the handsome flower spikes of Marram and Lyme Grass. As we climbed up onto the ridge of the first dunes, Ted pointed out some of the smaller plants that were colonising the bare patches of sand between the clumps of grass.

'The first of the smaller grasses to come into the Marram community is the Sand Fescue, *Festuca rubra* var. *arenaria*, a variety of the Red Fescue. And here is a sedge, the Sand Sedge, *Carex arenaria*. This has long creeping roots which often extend in straight lines and, as you can see, send up shoots at quite regular intervals. It occurs through much of the dune succession and frequently colonises areas in the later fixed dunes, where vegetation has been removed and the sand laid bare.

'It would be appropriate here to reflect on the subject of plant succession. Vegetation never stands still, it moves from one stage to another, as you can see if you neglect your garden for any length of time. This succession happens for a number of reasons, but the most important one is that the plants, in the early stages of colonisation, create conditions which will eventually be suitable for other plants but unsuitable for themselves. So in a sense they are signing their own death warrants by creating these new conditions. You can see the processes of succession on sand dunes more clearly than in almost any other habitat. We started on the outer dunes and we have already seen the way the dunes are being built up, although here they are still mobile with open areas. Gradually as we move further inland we shall find that the dunes are completely stable and that some of the plants of these early stages, even the powerful Marram Grass, have died out or become very reduced in vigour. Eventually we shall reach the climax of the succession, the position of greatest stability, which at Gibraltar Point is the Sea Buckthorn scrub, which we can see on the dunes further inland.

'If we look at some of the plants in the open patches around here, we can see that many of them are plants which do well on bare ground inland – field and garden weeds. We've seen Creeping Thistle, for example, and along there is a large patch of Corn Sowthistle. There are some docks and the very tall plants are Great Prickly Lettuce. At our feet is a little succulent plant with yellow flowers carpeting the ground – the Biting Stonecrop. Further inland we have a lot of

Ragwort and various hawkweeds and hawkbits. People often find their presence here surprising, but these are, after all, the conditions in which they flourish – open ground and lack of competition. Dunes must have been one of the few naturally disturbed habitats when most of the land was clothed in a dense cover of forest and other vegetation before the arrival of man with his axes and ploughs. Here, then, is probably one of the original homes of these weed species which were no doubt rarer in prehistoric times, than they are now.

'There is one plant here that is rather special and is highly characteristic of these

mobile dunes. It is the Sea Holly, *Eryngium maritimum*. The first thing you notice about it are these handsome bluish-green leaves with their very attractive veining. The leaves are quite tough and leathery. They have a waxy cuticle over the surface which reduces the loss of moisture. In addition, the leaf surface is reduced by having spiny points, like a holly leaf – hence the name. The flowers are over now but they are rather like those of Teasel – a very handsome bluish-purple. This is a perennial plant but it dies right down to the base in the autumn and the seeds are usually spread by the remains of the plant blowing away. It has an enor-

mously long tap root which can be over a metre long. Every winter it tends to be covered by the sand and in the spring it grows up through this. Here, erosion has exposed part of the root and you can see each year's growth and can measure how much sand was deposited during the winter.

'I had hoped to show you the beautiful Sea Bindweed, but the dune where it used to grow has been eroded away by winter storms; an indication of the very unstable conditions in these early mobile dunes. The Sea Bindweed copes with the changing surface by producing an extensive creeping mat of roots which help to stabilise its imme-

Being able to cope with the drying effect of the wind and the sun is one of the most important attributes amongst the sand dune life. Here two ladybirds are temporarily exposed searching for food amongst the seed heads of a Creeping Thistle (*Cirsium arvense*).

A Red-tailed Bumble-bee (*Bombus lapidarius*) feeding on a Sea Rocket flower.

diate environment. However, it is helpless against the ravages of a powerful winter's gale.

'On the underside of one of the leaves of this Sea Holly you can see a very nice banded snail. There are a lot of snails on these dunes and you may well ask where they get the calcium with which to build up their shells. The dunes are, in fact, quite rich in calcium – the sand itself has a certain amount of it and a lot of calcium is also derived from the shells of molluscs that have been washed up from the sea. In fact, a number of the plants growing here are lime-loving plants, calcicoles. When we look at the older dunes we will find a number of plants that frequently grow on chalk downs.

'The other day I spotted a thrush's anvil –

in this case, an old piece of tin where it could crack open the snail shells. You could see that the thrush had done very well – most of the shells were from the handsome banded snails. It is obviously difficult for a thrush to find somewhere hard where he can break the shells, so the rusty tin had been quite heavily used.

'Another interesting thing amongst the Marram Grass are these heaps of seeds. These are the remains of the meal of a Long-tailed Field Mouse, a common mammal in these dunes. And almost certainly the Kestrels which we can see hovering overhead are looking for these mice. There are also Short-tailed Voles around and these are the favourite prey of Short-eared Owls. These large day-flying owls can often be seen quartering the marsh. While we are out here on these fore-dunes it is worth looking for the Robber Fly. He is rather sinister-looking and stays absolutely stationary, crouching on the sand until another insect comes within range. When this happens he darts up and catches it in his strong front legs. He will then puncture his victim with his proboscis, which possibly contains a toxic substance as the victim collapses almost immediately. He then sucks it dry. Occasionally Robber Flies kill too many insects and then you will find that they impale some of their dead victims on the sharply pointed ends of Marram leaves.'

We had now arrived on the landward side of the first ridge of dunes where there was a

The sand dunes are rich in calcium and provide a home for many snails which need the calcium to build their shells. These snails provide a welcome source of food for hungry thrushes. But how do they break into the shells? This rusting tin can provided a handy anvil on which the thrush can smash the snails' shells.

Opposite **Sea Holly** (*Eryngium maritimum*) is one of the most striking seaside plants, with its teasel-like flower head and boldly veined holly-like leaves. A banded snail is hiding from the heat of the midday sun under one of its thick leaves.

The seeds of this Marram Grass have been stripped by a mouse who has left the remains of his dinner for all to see. With a bit of detective work you can often find the tracks of these small mammals criss-crossing over the dunes.

The large fly opposite is a Robber Fly waiting for another insect to come within range. It will then dart forward, capturing its prey with its strong front legs and then puncturing it with its pointed proboscis.

tidal lagoon. We found some more of the strand line wrack but here there was less Prickly Saltwort and only the occasional clump of Sea Rocket. Ted described the scene.

'The majority of the plants here obviously prefer quieter more stabilised conditions, although they have to be just as salt tolerant as those out on the fore-dunes. Even more so, in fact, because the tide flows into this lagoon. One of the most noticeable plants here is the Shrubby Seablite, a shrub which occurs along the edges of shingle beaches and sand dunes. It reaches a height of up to a metre and eventually forms a wide bush with many branches springing up from the stem. Its centre of distribution is the Mediterranean and it reaches its northern limit in the British Isles. In fact, the bushes here may possibly be the most northerly specimens in Europe!

'Looking inland from here we can see something very different from the sandy dune landscape we have just walked across. And to explain it we have to consider how these parallel ridges of dunes are formed. Out at sea you will often notice that the larger waves are breaking in shallow water and they are building up ridges of sand and shingle some distance from the main beach.

If a ridge of this kind becomes high enough it may stabilise and become an outer beach or offshore bar on which dunes can eventually develop. Between it and the shore the sea will still be able to flood in, forming a sheltered lagoon in which fine silts and mud will be deposited and on which saltmarsh will in time develop. This is what has happened here, which means that the dunes further inland, on the other side of this lagoon, were at one time the fore-shore. In fact, if we looked at old maps of this coastline we would see that it has been changing constantly in this way.

'We can walk down just a few feet from these sand dunes and have a look at the saltmarsh vegetation. We do not find the clear zonation that you have on a frontal saltmarsh directly open to the sea, but we can observe the early stages of colonisation. Saltmarsh plants have to live in a very difficult habitat, even more harsh, in a way, than the sand dunes, because although there is plenty of water, it is saltwater. The ways in which they have overcome this salt problem are fairly complex but to put it very simply, plants derive their water from the soil by exerting a form of suction pressure (called "osmotic pressure") in the roots which draws the water in. Now, if you put a garden plant into saltmarsh it would wilt and die in next to no time but these plants have adapted to growing in saltmarshes by, amongst other things, exerting a much greater suction pressure to overcome the effect of the salt in the soil. It is, perhaps, not surprising that few plants have managed to adapt to this terrain and it is therefore a very simple habitat in terms of plant composition. However, when you get to the edges of the marsh the conditions are not so extreme and if we walk along we will be able to see quite a variety of plants of the dune saltmarsh edge.

'Let's look at a conspicuous one first of all. This low shrubby plant with these grey spoon-shaped leaves and small yellow flowers is called Sea Purslane, *Halimione portulacoides*. It likes to grow in fairly well-drained places on the saltmarsh, hence it is on the edge here and you will also find it commonly on the banks of the creeks. It is a very good silt collector with its sprawling habit. It has an extraordinary leathery texture and if you look at it through a hand lens you can see that it is covered with a dense coat of fine hairs – another adaptation to prevent too much water loss.

'Then there is this rather pretty little plant with star-like pinkish flowers. This is the Greater Sea Spurrey which is quite abundant along saltmarsh edges.

'Further along here are two more plants of this saltmarsh fringe – Sea Milkwort and Sea Heath. The little prostrate plant with the oval leaves crowded along the stems radiating from a central rootstock, is the Sea Milkwort, *Glaux maritima*. It has pretty pink flowers in the axils of the leaves in May and June and occurs all round the coast of Britain. Sea Heath, *Frankenia laevis*, on the other hand, is much more localised; it occurs only on the south and east coasts of England and is at the very northern limit of its range here. It is a little shrubby plant which grows quite flat against the ground, sending out

these long trailing stems, which eventually root down and extend the mat. The stems are an attractive reddish colour and it has small pink flowers.

Moving out now onto more open saltmarsh we have a lovely plant – the sea lavender. The species that grows just here – rather inappropriately named for this situation – is the Rock Sea Lavender, *Limonium binervosum*. It grows here on the slightly drier edges of the saltmarsh and is a more slender plant with smaller leaves than the Common Sea Lavender, *Limonium vulgare*, which carpets large areas of saltmarsh.

'If we walk further out into the muddy areas we cross over a zone of almost pure Sea Meadow Grass, *Puccinellia maritima* – a

Behind the first ridge of dunes is a saltmarsh lagoon. This is a plant which is typical of saltmarsh edges – Sea Purslane (*Halimone portulacoides*).

blind King Lear:

"The crows and choughs that wing the
    midway air
Show scarce so gross as beetles; half
    way down
Hangs one that gathers sampire,
    dreadful trade!
Methinks he seems no bigger than his
    head."

People who come here and see this samphire are very puzzled by that reference, but that is, of course, the Rock Samphire which is also gathered for food. Perhaps, it is best to call it by its other name, Glasswort, which refers to its use, like the Prickly Saltwort, as providing soda for making glass.

'The important point about Glasswort is its role in colonising bare mud. You can see if I pull up a plant, that it has a surprisingly long root with which to anchor itself in the mobile mud. It has probably been covered by several fresh layers of silt and has continued to come up through them. The plant consists mainly of jointed sections of stem with tiny scale-like leaves at the base of the joints from which numerous branches arise. The flowers have these tiny yellow anthers but they produce vast quantities of seeds which when it has died off are found all the way up the stem. These seeds provide an important winter source of food for large numbers of finches and other seed-eating birds, such as the handsome Snow Buntings which spend the winter here. The remaining seed is washed out by the tides, distributing the plant along the coast.

    Here is the other of these early annual

Above **Lesser Sea Spurrey** (*Spergularia maritima*) – **a common saltmarsh plant.**

Right **Glasswort** (*Salicornia europaea*) **one of the first colonisers of saltmarshes. This extraordinary little plant shows several adaptations to this inhospitable terrain – reduced scale-like leaves, succulent stems and tiny flowers. Its extensive root system helps bind the saltmarsh muds and silts.**

low growing plant with prostrate stems which spread out to form a great mat. It forms a fine springy turf and where it is abundant it forms extensive grazing marshes. Here it is heavily grazed by rabbits.

'Here is a little bit of a creek that has left a bare expanse of mud and this is where we can see the two first colonists of saltmarshes apart from the vigorous cordgrasses which dominate the early zones of some marshes. This one is called Marsh Samphire or Glasswort, *Salicornia europaea*, along these coasts and it used to be regarded as quite an attractive dish, either boiled or pickled in vinegar. It is not to be confused with the Rock Samphire which belongs to quite a different family of plants, the Umbelliferae, and grows on cliffs. There is a passage in Shakespeare's *King Lear* where Edmund describes an imaginary view down a cliff face to the

colonists. This is the Annual Sea Blite, *Suaeda maritima*, which like the Glasswort is a succulent type of plant. It is usually prostrate, but where it grows in a dense sward with the Glasswort it tends to be more upright. It too has tiny flowers and produces abundant seed. Like Glasswort it plays an important role in arresting silt and mud and so building up the level of the marsh until the Sea Meadow Grass and plants like the

Sea Aster and the Common Sea Lavender can get going.'

From this saltmarsh lagoon and the foredunes we wound our way inland towards the older more stable dunes. The vegetation on these was markedly different, as Ted explained.

'We have moved inland now onto an older dune ridge where the vegetation cover is complete. Below us are mosses which are

The masses of delicate pink flowers of the sea lavenders are one of the most impressive sites on our late-summer saltmarshes. These plants are Rock Sea Lavender (*Limonium binervosum*), but the most common sea lavender is *L. vulgare*.

Above **A covering of mosses and lichens on the stabilised dunes. These are character-istic of the more open areas of these old dunes giving them a grey appearance, hence the name 'grey dunes'.**

Right **Some plants, more typical as arable weeds inland, colonise the more sheltered areas of the dune system. Here Ragwort (** *Senecio jacobaea* **), a common weed, has established itself amongst the Dewberry and Sea Buckthorn.**

some of the most efficient plants in fixing the surface of the sand once it is sufficiently stabilised for them to grow. There are several species characteristic of the early fixed dune stage, the most universal of which is *Tortula ruraliformis*. Another im-portant moss is *Camptothecium lutescens*. Both have folded leaves with rolled-back margins, which are protective devices that help them to survive in dry periods. On dunes such as this, lichens also play an im-portant part in covering the surface and they too, although becoming considerably shri-velled, are able to survive long dry spells. The two main types that grow here are *Cladonia* and *Peltigera* species, both of which are common on sand dunes. Where they grow thickly they give a grey colouring to the dunes and these are often then referred to as "grey dunes" as distinct from the younger, mobile "yellow dunes" where bare sand is still conspicuous.

'These fixed dunes have a greater variety of plants and some of the early colonists still survive here – we can see small non-flower-ing clumps of Marram Grass and Sand Sedge, which is rejuvenated as soon as a patch of sand is laid bare. However, most of the plants are now no longer exclusively

seaside species. Over there are the stems of Ragwort. They have been stripped of their leaves by the caterpillars of the Cinnabar Moth, which have bright black and yellow bands around their bodies, rather like a football jersey. The moth itself is scarlet and black and rather weak flying. Both the moth and the caterpillar are distasteful to birds and they use this bright warning coloration to make sure the birds don't forget once they have tasted one.

'Growing low to the ground we have the familiar Scarlet Pimpernel and here is Black Nightshade. Another common plant here is Hound's Tongue, which at this time of year has masses of seeds with little hooked spines that stick to your clothes.

'Covering the surface of a great deal of the dune is this creeping relative of the Black-berry – Dewberry, *Rubus caesius*. It sends out long stems which root down and has these distinctive fruits with a rather plum-like bloom to them. In the sheltered hollows in these stable dunes you can find a lot of interesting small plants such as the little Mouse-eared Chickweed, Thyme-leaved Sandwort, Early Forget-me-not, Rue-leaved Saxifrage as well as various tares and vetches. They make miniature gardens when they are at their best in April and May. One of the more striking plants that you can find here is the Viper's Bugloss with its tall spikes of blue flowers; this is a typical plant also of the chalklands.

'If the vegetation here is not restricted by grazing or mowing it will "climax" into scrub. All around us we can see this climax vegetation in the form of a handsome shrub called Sea Buckthorn, *Hippophae rham-noides*. It is native along the east coast of England, but has been planted in many dune areas in the south and west. It has silvery-grey leaves and is protected by wickedly sharp spines which effectively deter rabbits from eating all but the youngest shoots. The undersides of the leaves, incidentally, have a dense covering of silvery-white scales, which is yet another development to check trans-piration. Sea Buckthorn has separate male and female plants and, since it spreads mainly by means of powerful underground runners, plants of the same sex occur to-gether. This is most clear when the bright orange berries ripen on the female bushes, which they are just beginning to do now. They are at their best in October and

Below left **Dewberry** (*Rubus caesius*) **showing its distinctive fruits with their plum-like bloom. This plant sends out 'runners' across the stable dunes.**

Below **A view across from the Sea Buck-thorn covered dunes to the 'yellow' dunes of the foreshore with areas of saltmarsh in-between. The succession from the open sandy beach to the high scrub-covered dunes can be seen all around our coast where suitable conditions prevail. So pick your way with care next time you cross a landscape like this – you will be amazed what you will discover.**

The bright orange berries of Sea Buckthorn (*Hippophae rhamnoides*) amongst the distinctive silvery-grey leaves. These berries provide a feast for visiting winter thrushes in the late autumn and provide an eye-catching show of colour during an autumn stroll in the sand dunes.

November and during this time they form a very important food supply for migrant thrushes, particularly Fieldfares from Scandinavia. As you can see it forms a dense thicket up to three metres high.

There are other shrubs in this zone and by the path here is a venerable old Elder covered with lichens. There is also Hawthorn and Wild Privet, and Dog Rose. All this dense scrub provides a marvellous area for nesting birds. Whitethroats, Sedge Warblers, Linnets, Dunnocks and Yellowhammers are all common here. Later in the year on a favourable day in late summer or autumn the bushes are often alive with

migratory birds, moving south along the coast.

'The sheltered open areas in the scrub are also good places for quite a variety of butterflies such as the Meadow Brown and the Hedge Brown, the Small Heath and the Small Copper, as well as immigrants such as the Red Admiral and the Painted Lady.'

Before we made our way home Ted pointed out some of the ways in which sand dunes have been developed and some of the pressures that are threatening them.

'Where there are woodlands near the coast, sand dunes have often been invaded by tree species and many dune areas have

been planted with Scots and other pines. Because they have the right kinds of contours and are well drained with a fine short turf some sand dunes are much sought after as golf-courses, which incidentally, are often very good places for flowers, especially in the "roughs". The dunes are also, of course, very popular with seaside holidaymakers and on some parts of the coast this has led to serious erosion problems as the dunes are very unstable, as we have seen, and will not withstand a lot of trampling.'

At Gibraltar Point the paths through the dunes were clearly marked and often laid with old railway sleepers, keeping erosion by the visitors to a minimum. It had been a real pleasure out walking with Ted Smith and we had seen a vast spectrum of seaside plants and animals, yet we had only scratched the surface. How different it must all be in depths of winter when the Marram has turned a delicate straw colour and the dunes are white with snow, and flocks of Snow Buntings are feeding out on the dunes. Or in spring when a whole range of different plants are in flower and the warblers are singing from the Sea Buckthorn thicket. It had certainly been shown to us that there is a fascinating world to discover amongst the dunes.

A Small Copper Butterfly (*Lycaena phlaeas*), feeding on Ragwort in a sunny dune hollow. During a good summer this butterfly may produce three generations and can be seen on the wing from April right through to October.

Further reading

Barret, J. and Yonge, C. M., *Collins Pocket Guide to the Sea Shore*, Collins (1972).

Barrett, J. and Ovenden, D., *Collins Handguide to the Sea Coast*, Collins (1981).

Bellamy, D. J., *Bellamy's Britain*, BBC Publications (1974).

Bellamy, D. J., *The Life-giving Sea*, Hamish Hamilton (1975).

Bellamy, D. J., *Botanic Man*, Hamlyn (1978).

Bruun, B. and Singer, A., *The Hamlyn Guide to Birds of Britain and Europe*, Hamlyn (1970, revised 1978).

Campbell, A. C. and Nicholls, J., *The Hamlyn Guide to the Seashore and Shallow Seas of Britain and Europe*, Hamlyn (1976).

Chinery, M., *A Field Guide to the Insects of Britain and Northern Europe*, Collins (1973).

Corbet, G. B. and Southern, H. N. (eds.), *The Handbook of British Mammals*, Blackwell (1977).

Hepburn, I., *Flowers of the Coast*, Collins (1952).

Holliday, F. G. T., *Wildlife of Scotland*, Macmillan (1979).

Hubbard, C. E., *Grasses*, Penguin (1968).

Morris, P. (ed.), *The Natural History of the British Isles*, Country Life (1979).

Nelson, B., *Seabirds – their biology and ecology*, Hamlyn (1979).

Ogilvie, M. A., *Bird-watcher's Guide to the Wetlands of Britain*, Batsford (1979).

Ranwell, D. S., *Ecology of Salt Marshes and Sand Dunes*, Chapman and Hall (1972).

Rose, F., *Wildflower Key*, Warne (1981).

Prater, A. J., *Estuary Birds of Britain and Ireland*, Poyser (1981).

Yonge, C. M., *The Sea Shore*, Collins (1949; Fontana ed. 1971).

Organisations to join

Botanical Society of the British Isles
68 Outwoods Road, Loughborough, Leicestershire.
A national society for both amateur and professional botanists. Organises mapping schemes and is active in the conservation of our wild plants.

British Butterfly Conservation Society
Tudor House, Quorn, Leicester.

British Trust for Conservation Volunteers
10-14 Duke Street, Reading, Berkshire RG1 4RU.
An organisation for people over sixteen years of age which undertakes practical projects, such as clearing scrub, maintaining reserves, tree-planting, etc.

British Trust for Ornithology
Beech Grove, Tring, Hertfordshire.
National organisation which carries out research into all aspects of bird life supported by a growing army of amateur enthusiasts.

Ramblers' Association
1-5 Wandsworth Road, London SW8 2LJ.

Royal Society for Nature Conservation
The Green, Nettleham, Lincoln.
The Royal Society for Nature Conservation is the national association of the 42 local Nature Conservation Trusts which forms the major voluntary organisation concerned with all aspects of wildlife conservation in the United Kingdom. The Trusts have a combined membership of 140,000 and, together with the Society, own or manage 1,300 nature reserves throughout the UK covering a range of sites, from woodland and heathland to wetland and estuarine habitats. Most Trusts have full-time staff but the members themselves, with a wide range of skills, contribute greatly to all aspects of the work.

RSPB, Royal Society for the Protection of Birds
The Lodge, Sandy, Bedfordshire.
The major conservation organisation for birds and their habitats.

The Scottish Wildlife Trust
25 Johnston Terrace, Edinburgh EH1 2NH.
The Scottish branch of the County Conservation Trusts.

Watch: The Watch Trust for Environmental Education
22 The Green, Nettleham, Lincoln LN2 2NR.
Junior section of the RSNC.

Wildfowl Trust
Slimbridge, Gloucester GL2 7BT.

World Wildlife Fund
29 Greville Street, London EC1N 8AX.

Index

Figures in italics refer to illustrations.

Places of interest around our coast

see Information pages for further details

1 Westray, Orkneys
2 North Hoy, Orkneys
3 Dunnet Head, Scottish Highlands
4 Dornoch Firth, Scottish Highlands
5 Cromarty Firth, Scottish Highlands
6 Culbin Sands, Grampian
7 Sands of Forvie, Grampian
8 Tentsmuir Point, Fife
9 Bass Rock, Lothian
10 St Abbs Head, Borders
11 Lindisfarne, Northumberland
12 Farne Islands, Northumberland
13 Teeside, Cleveland
14 Flamborough Head and Bempton Cliffs, Humberside
15 Spurn Point, Humberside
16 Gibraltar Point, Lincolnshire
17 Wash, Lincolnshire/Norfolk
18 Hunstanton, Norfolk
19 Scolt Head, Norfolk
20 Blakeney Point, Norfolk
21 Orfordness, Suffolk
22 Walton-on-the-Naze, Essex
23 North Kent Marshes, Kent
24 Sandwich Bay, Kent

25 Dungeness, Kent
26 Beachy Head, Sussex
27 Seven Sisters, Sussex
28 Portsmouth, Langstone, Chichester Harbours, Hampshire/Sussex
29 Hurst Point, Hampshire
30 The Needles, Isle of Wight
31 Purbeck Cliffs, Dorset
32 Lulworth Cove, Dorset
33 Chesil Beach, Dorset
34 Exe Estuary, Devon
35 Dawlish Warren, Devon
36 Slapton Sands, Devon
37 Start Point, Devon
38 Fal Estuary, Cornwall
39 Lizard, Cornwall
40 Cornwall Coast Path, Cornwall
41 Bude, Cornwall
42 Welcombe and Marshland Reserve, Devon
43 Braunton Burrows, Devon
44 Bridgwater Bay, Somerset
45 Slimbridge, Gloucester
46 Dunraven, Glamorgan
47 Gower Peninsula, Glamorgan
48 Whiteford Burrows, Glamorgan
49 Pembroke Coast Path, Dyfed

50 Skomer Island, Dyfed
51 St Davids Head, Dyfed
52 Cors Fochno, Dyfed
53 Newborough Warren, Gwynedd
54 Menai Straits, Gwynedd
55 South Stack, Gwynedd
56 Dee Estuary, Clwyd/Merseyside
57 Ainsdale, Merseyside
58 Morecambe Bay, Lancashire/Cumbria
59 St Bees Head, Cumbria
60 Caerlaverock, Dumfries
61 Mull of Galloway, Galloway
62 South Ardnamurchan Coast, Argyll
63 Loch Scavaig, Skye
64 Giant's Causeway, Antrim
65 Dingle Bay, Kerry